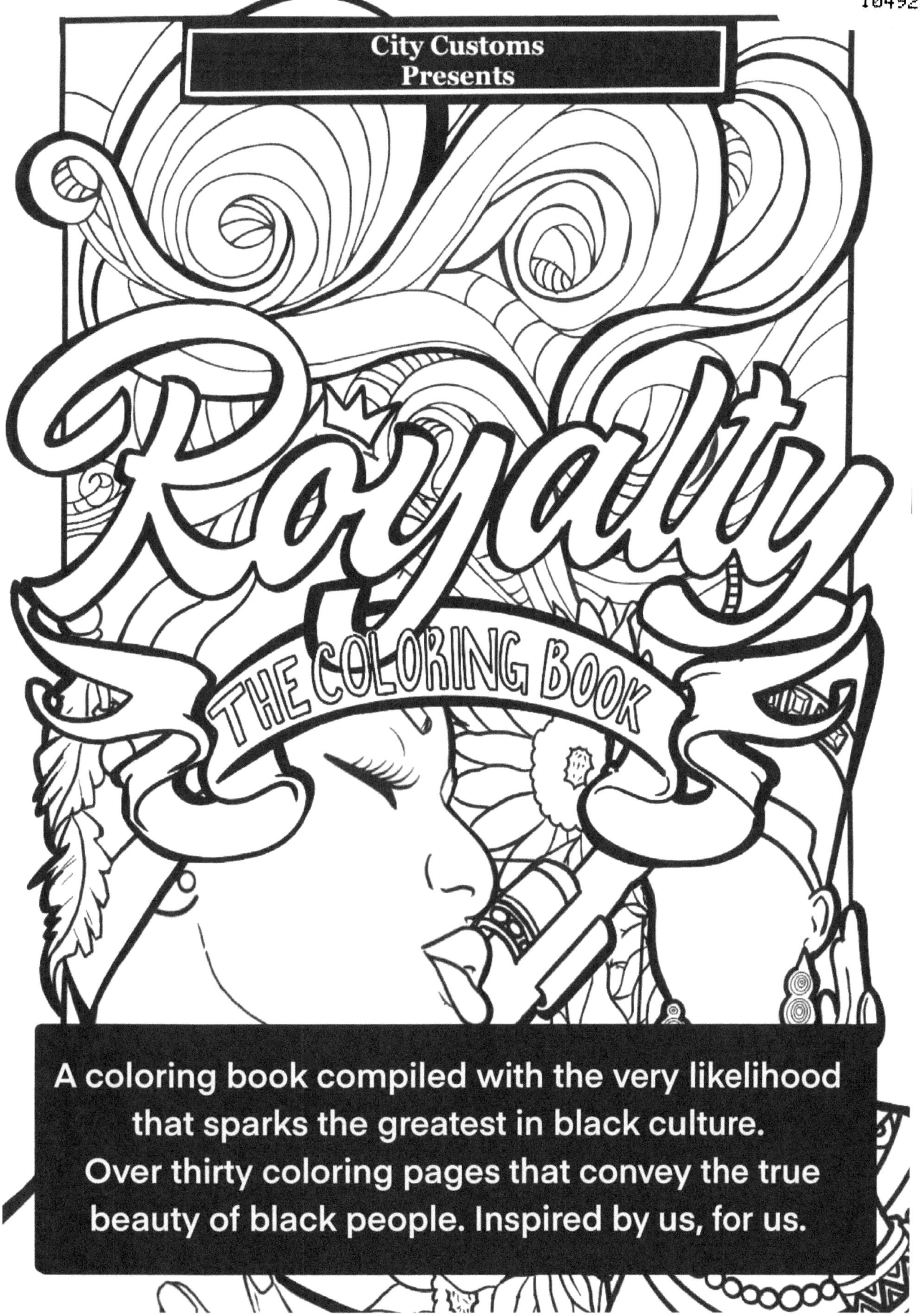

**City Customs
Presents**

Royalty

THE COLORING BOOK

A coloring book compiled with the very likelihood that sparks the greatest in black culture. Over thirty coloring pages that convey the true beauty of black people. Inspired by us, for us.

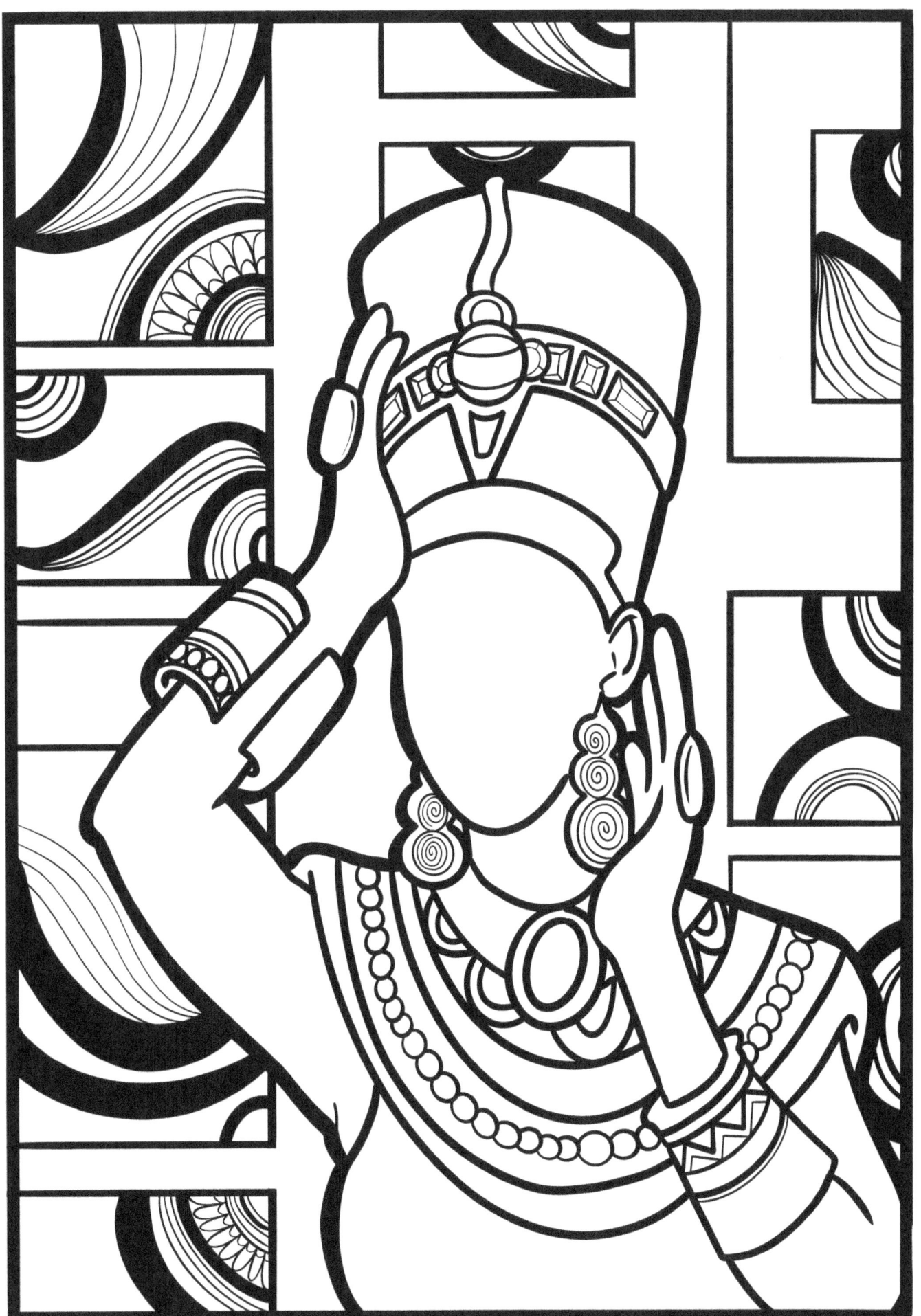

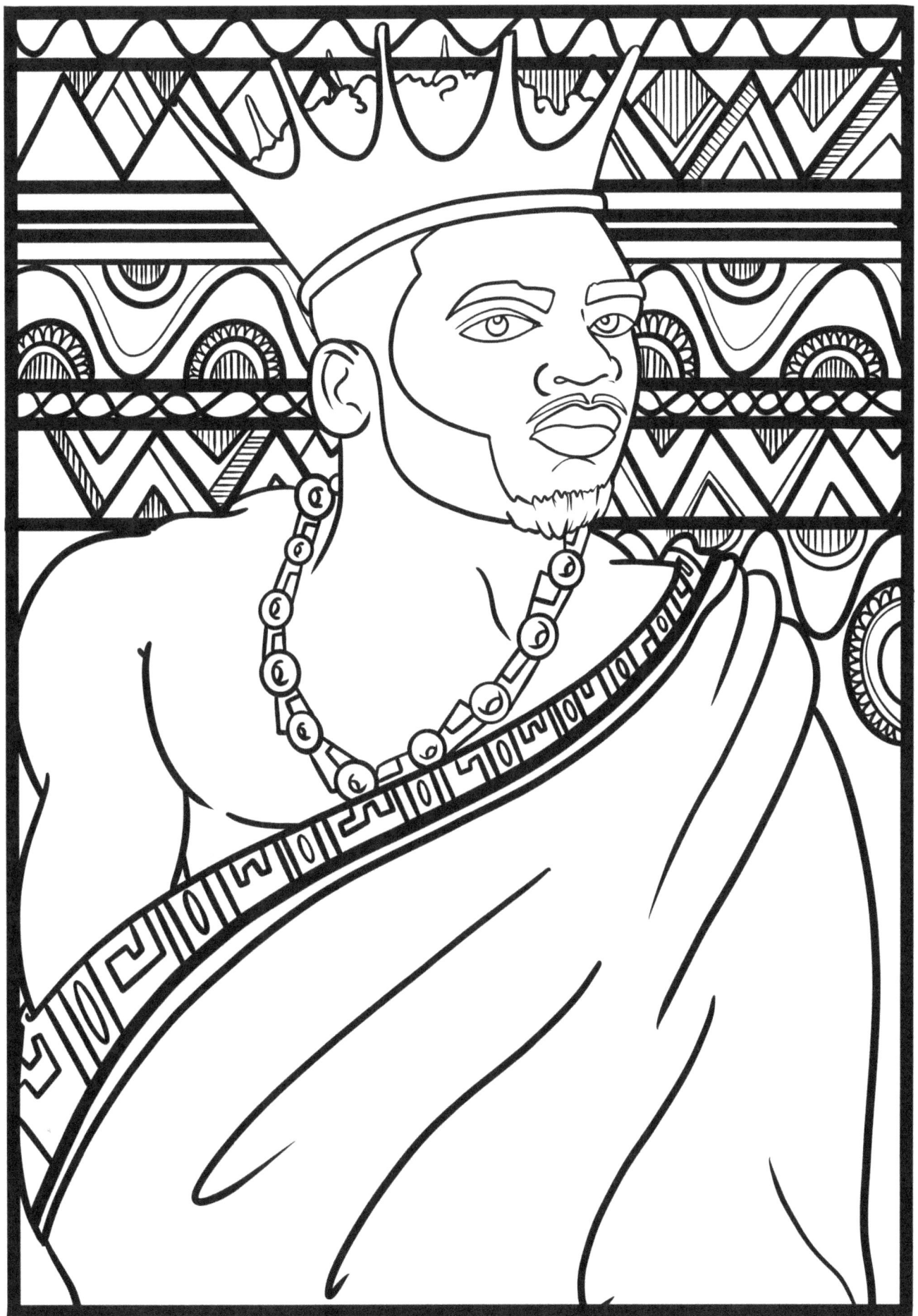

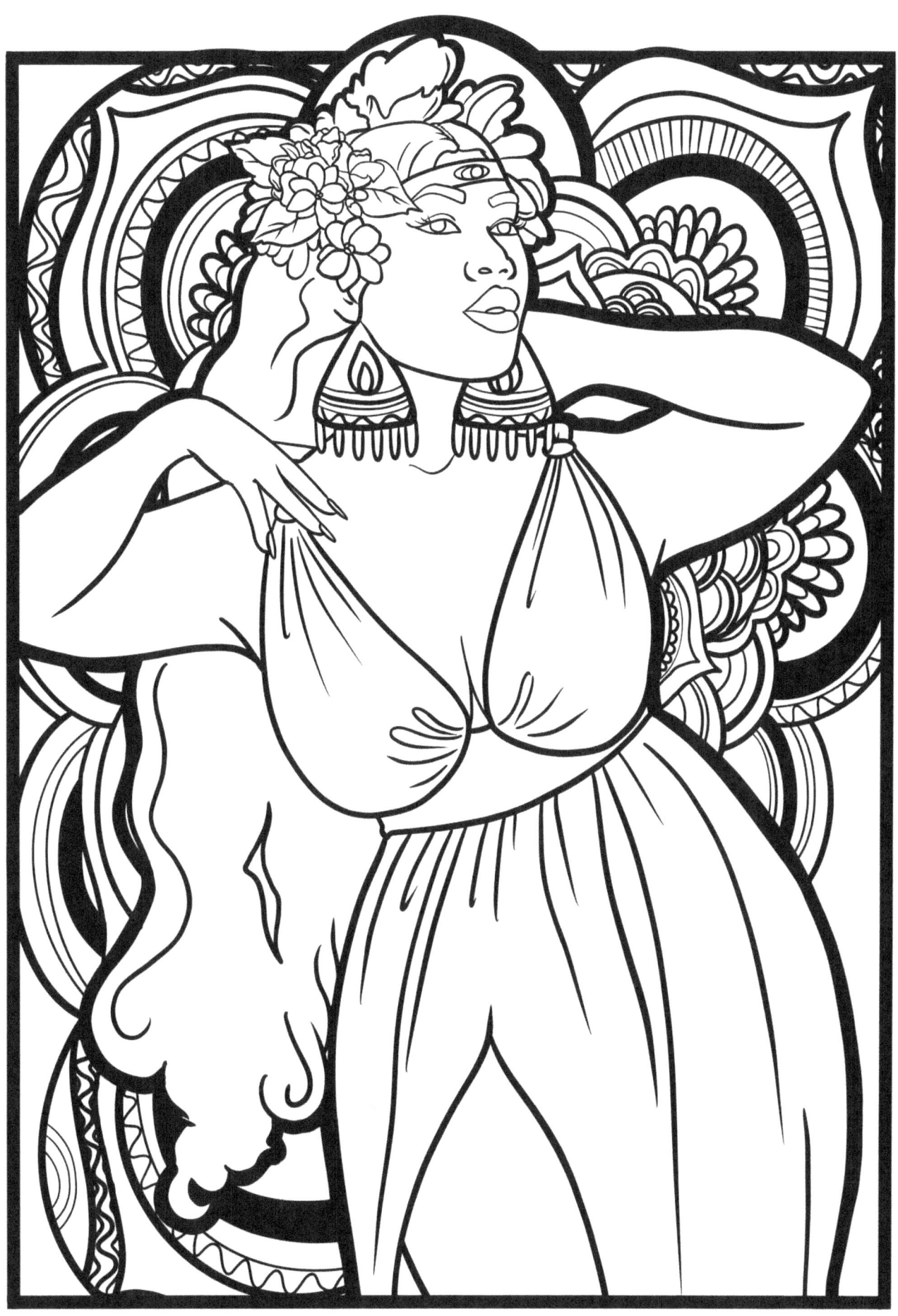

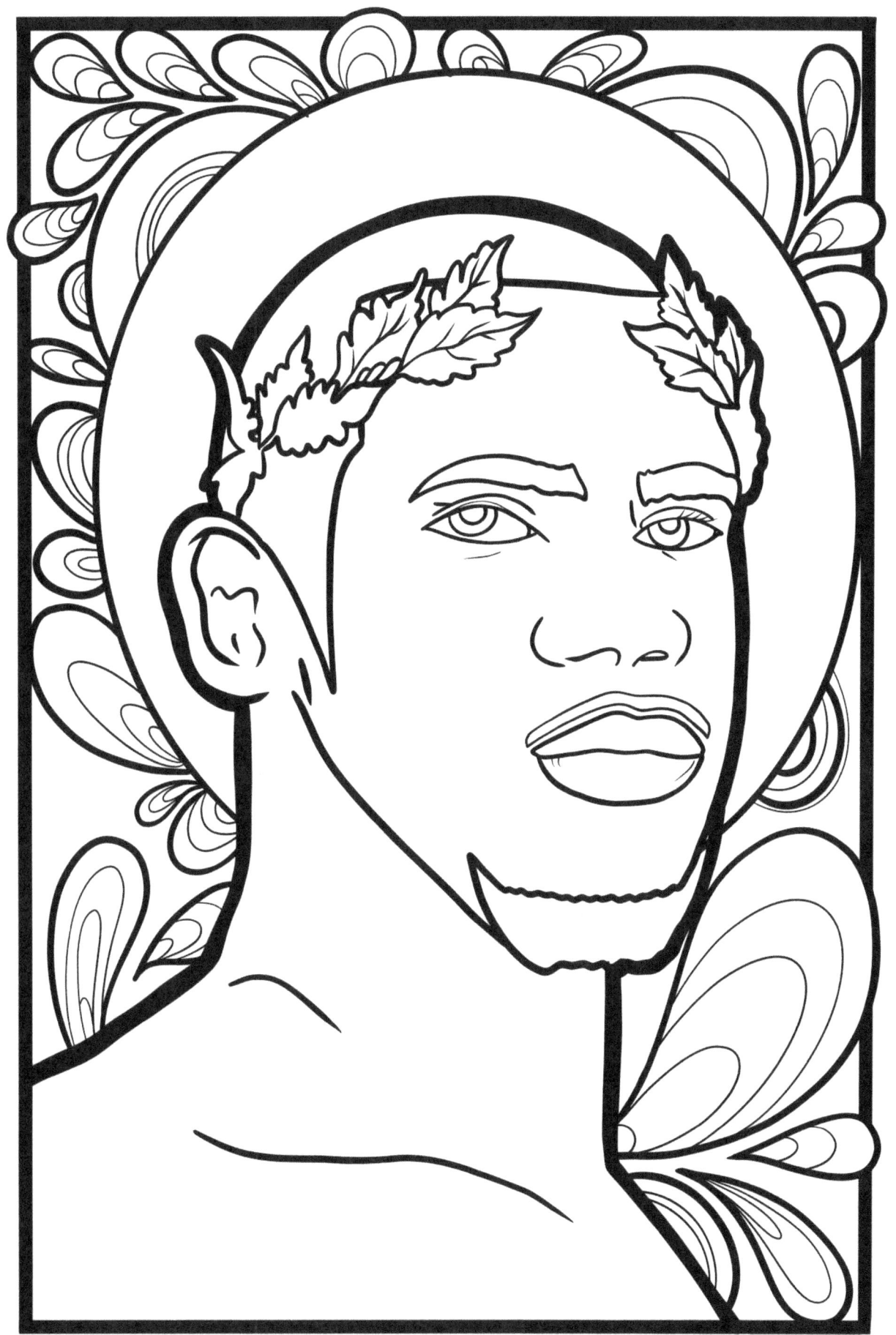

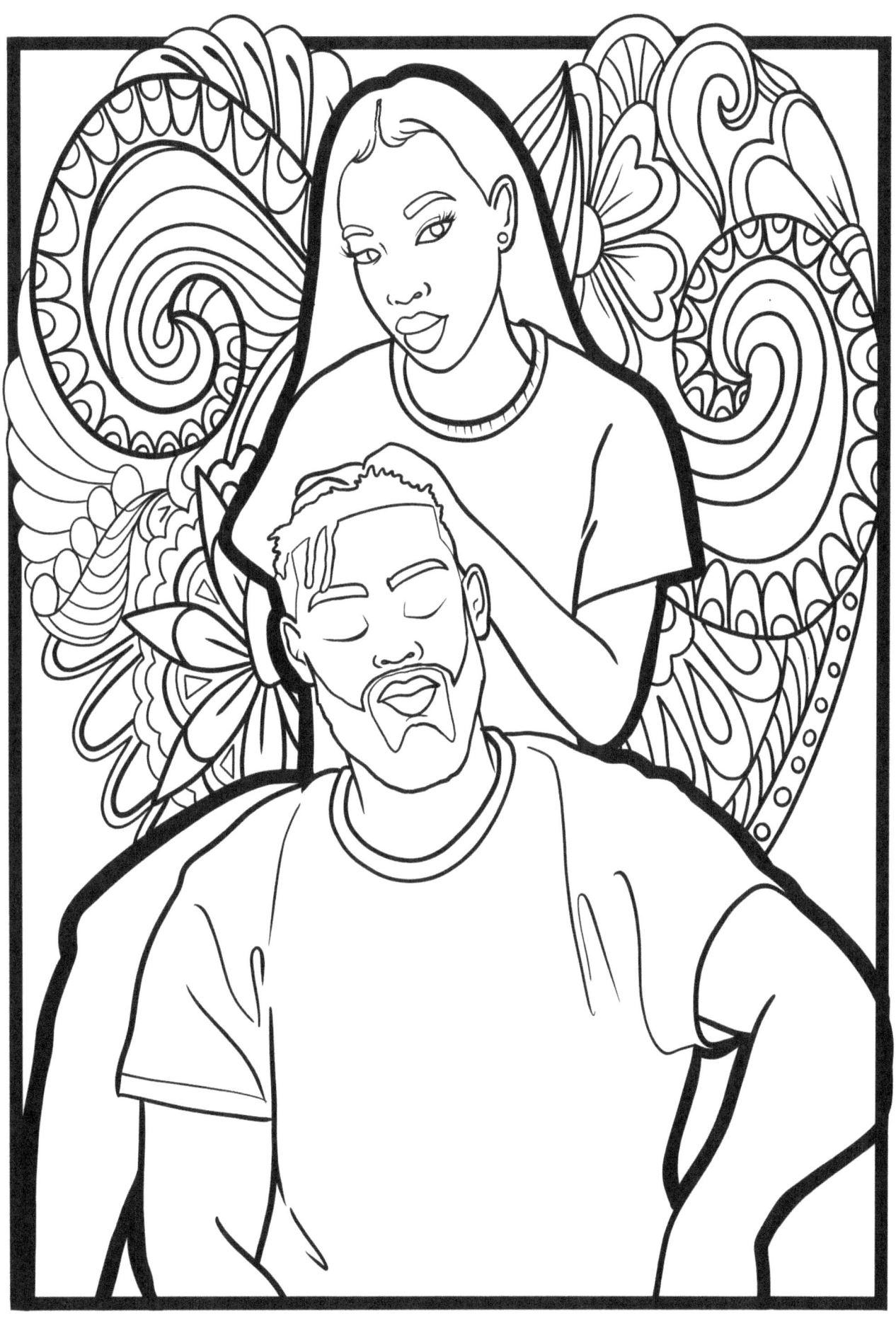

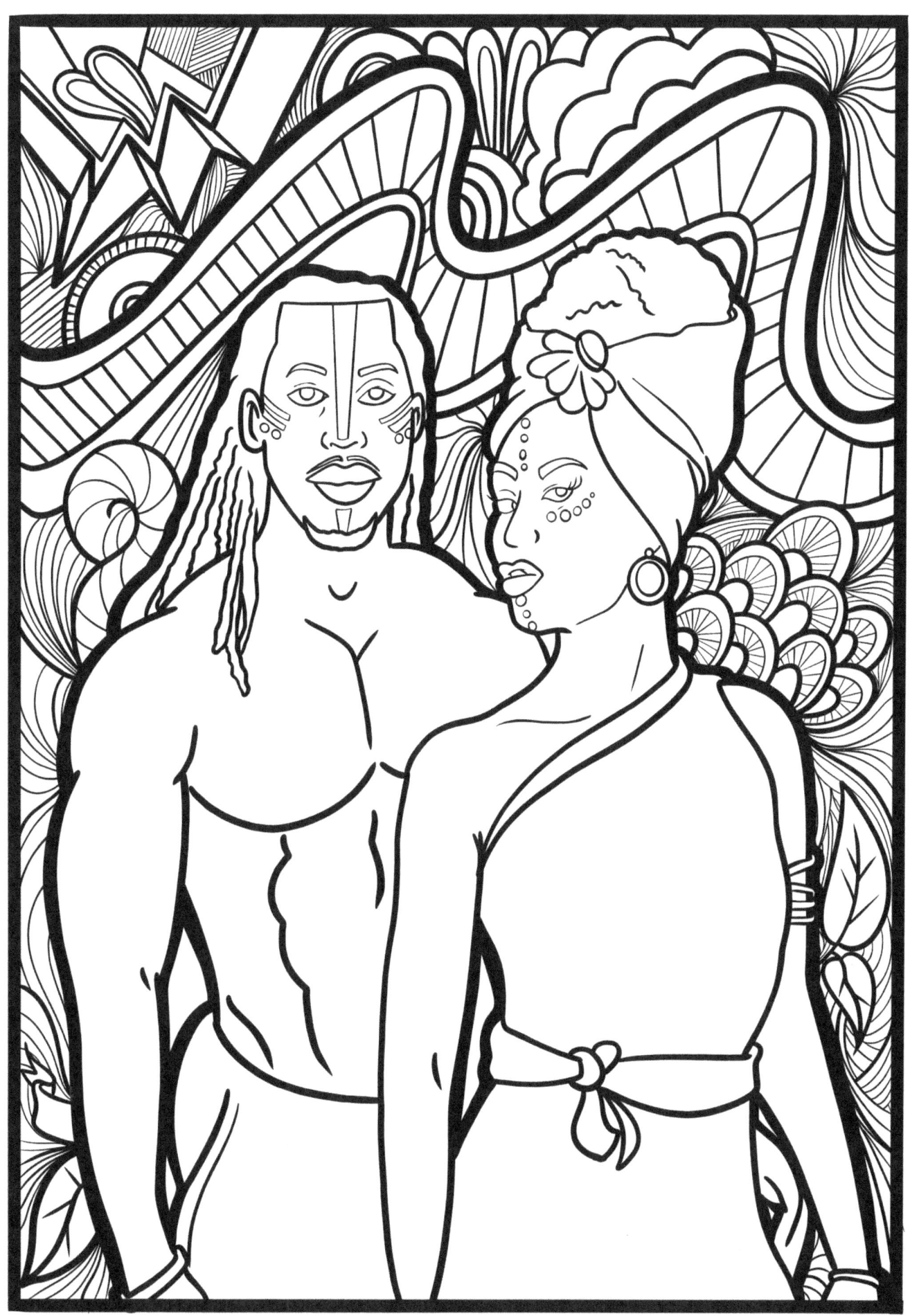

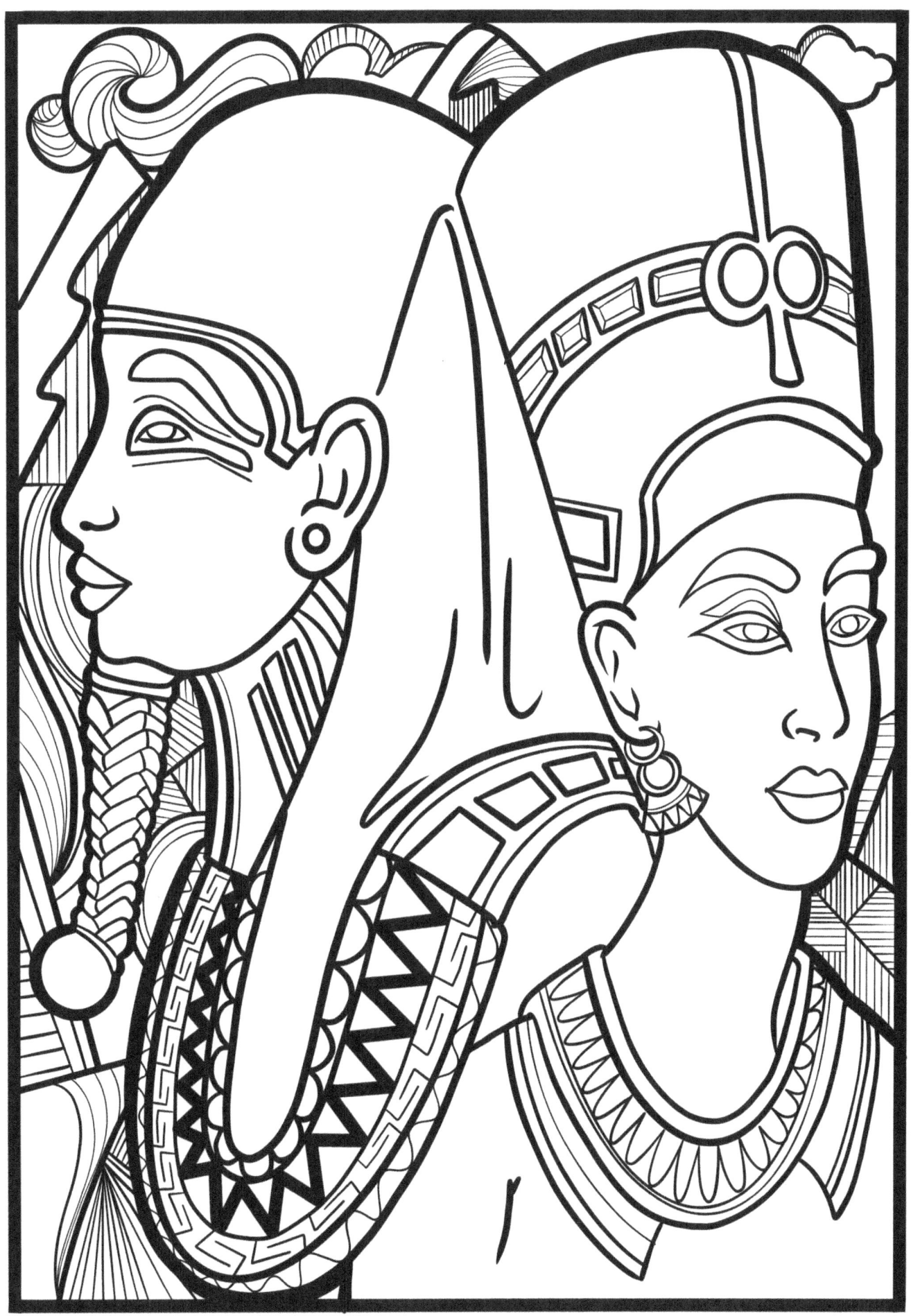

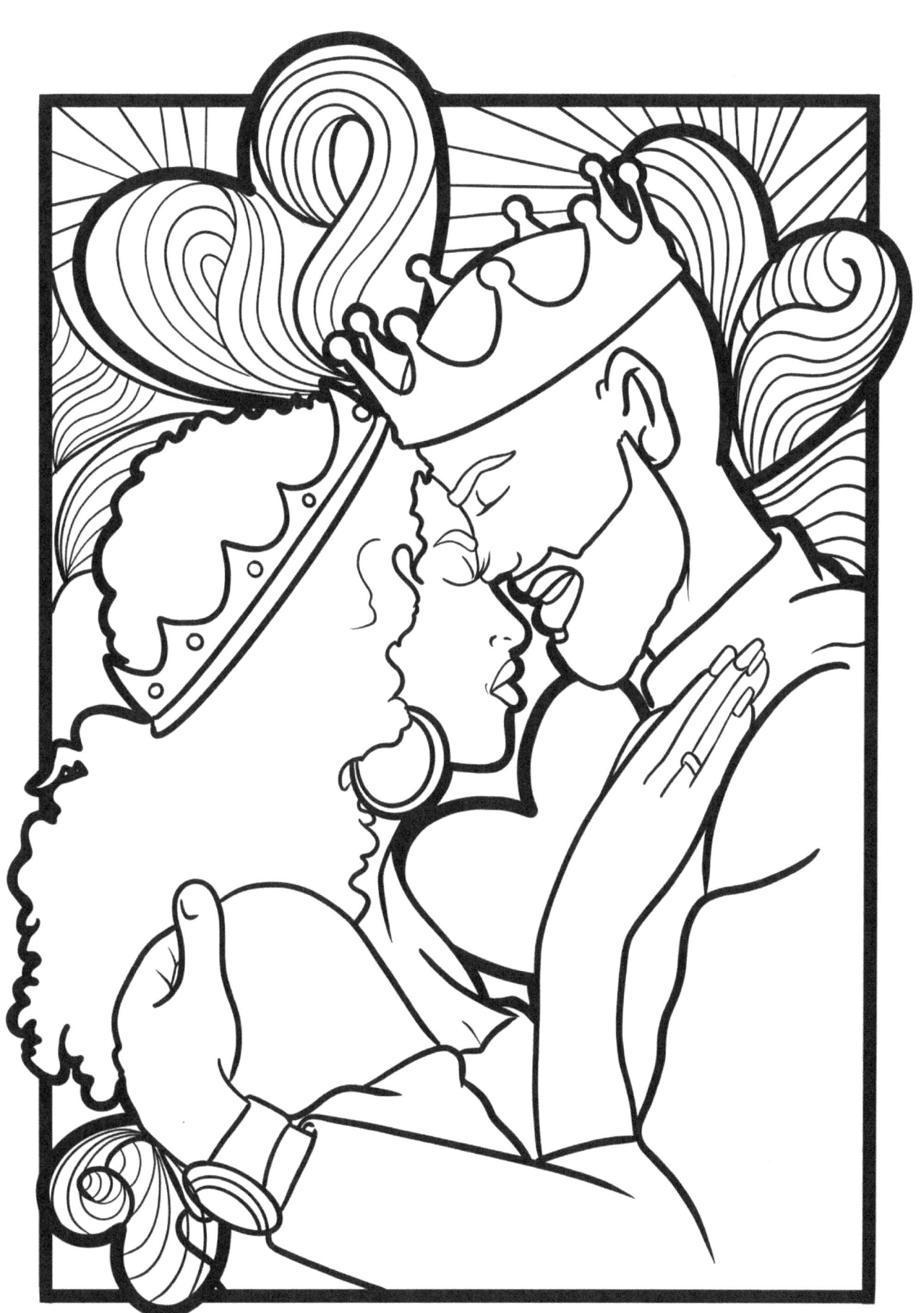

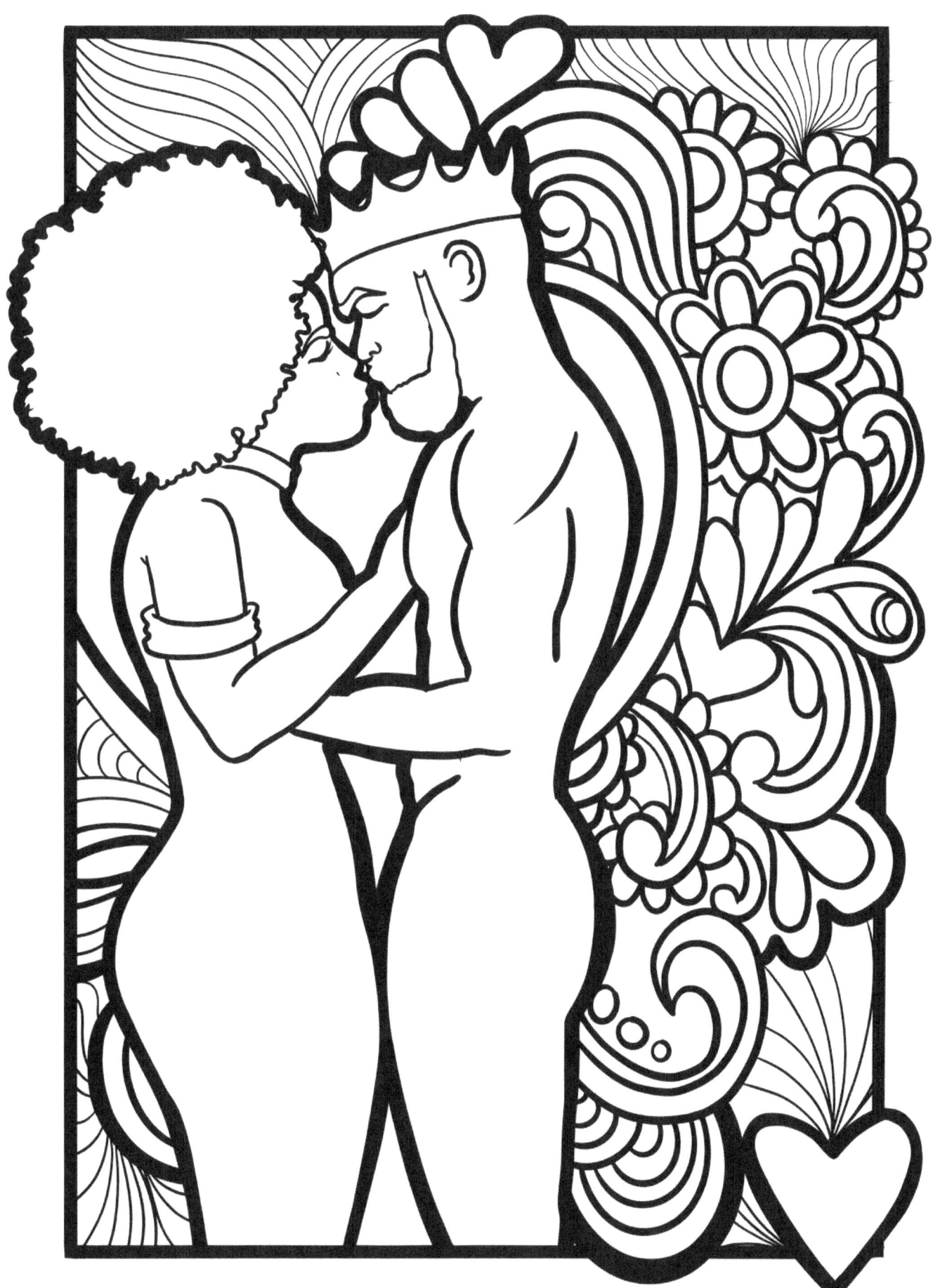

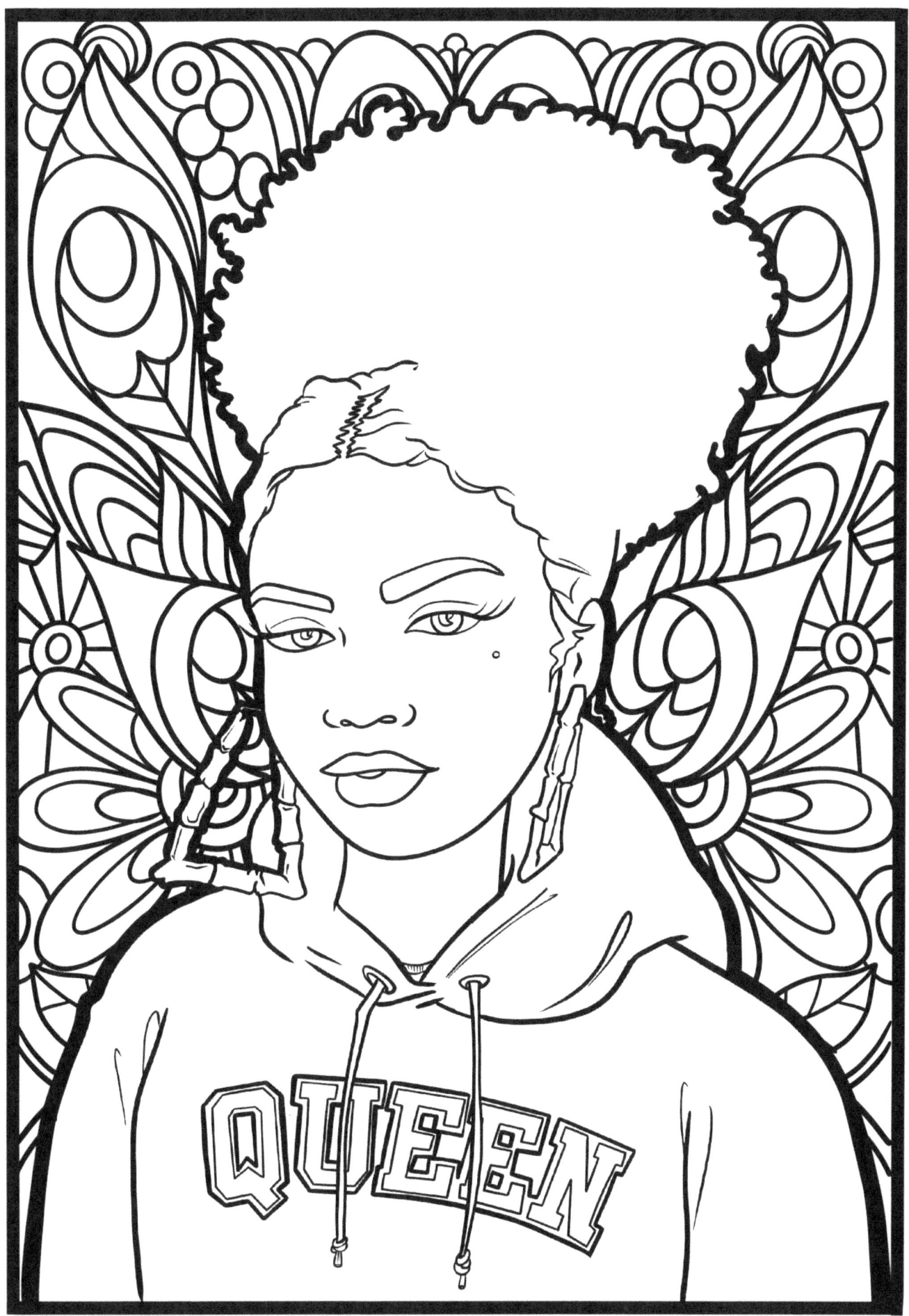

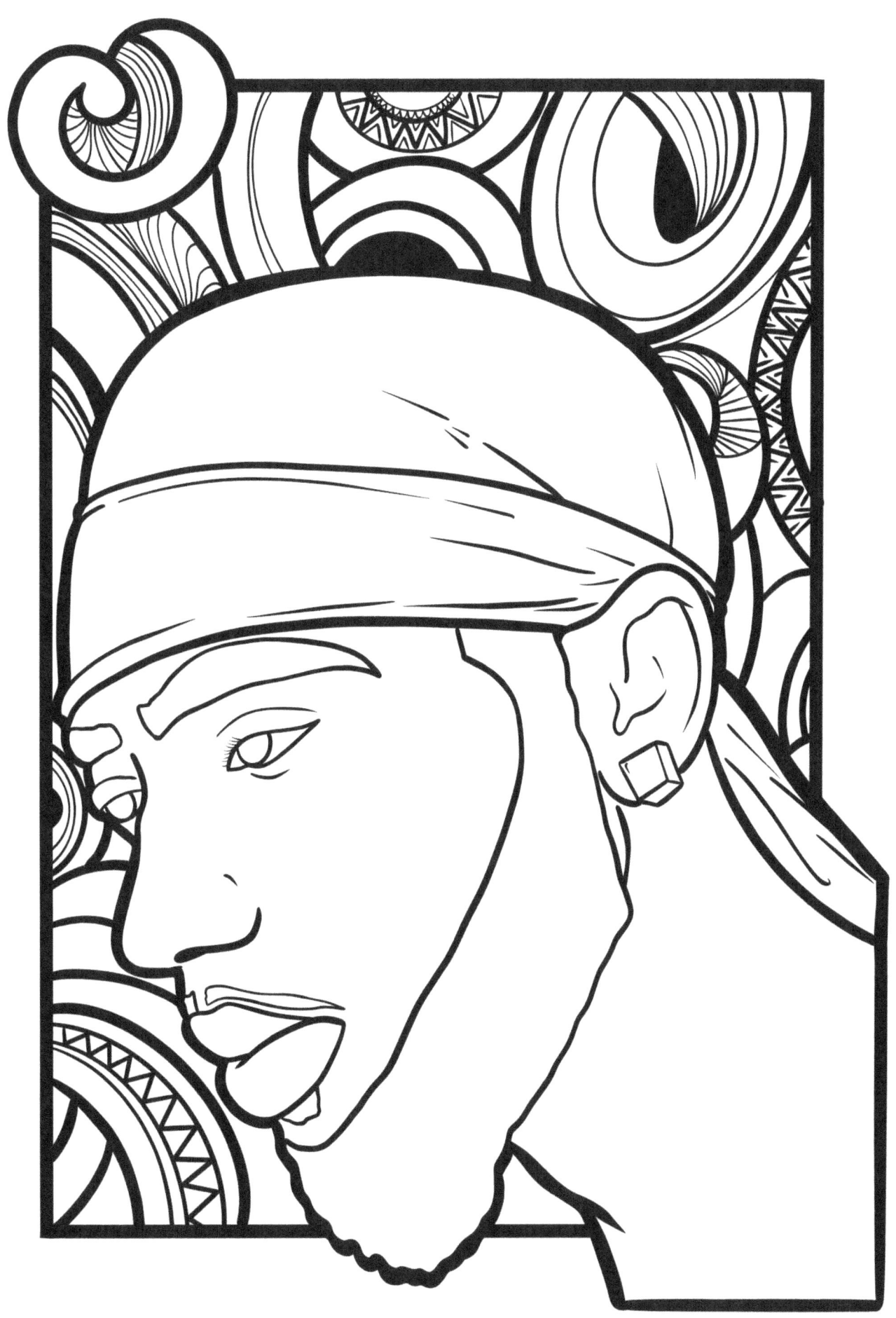

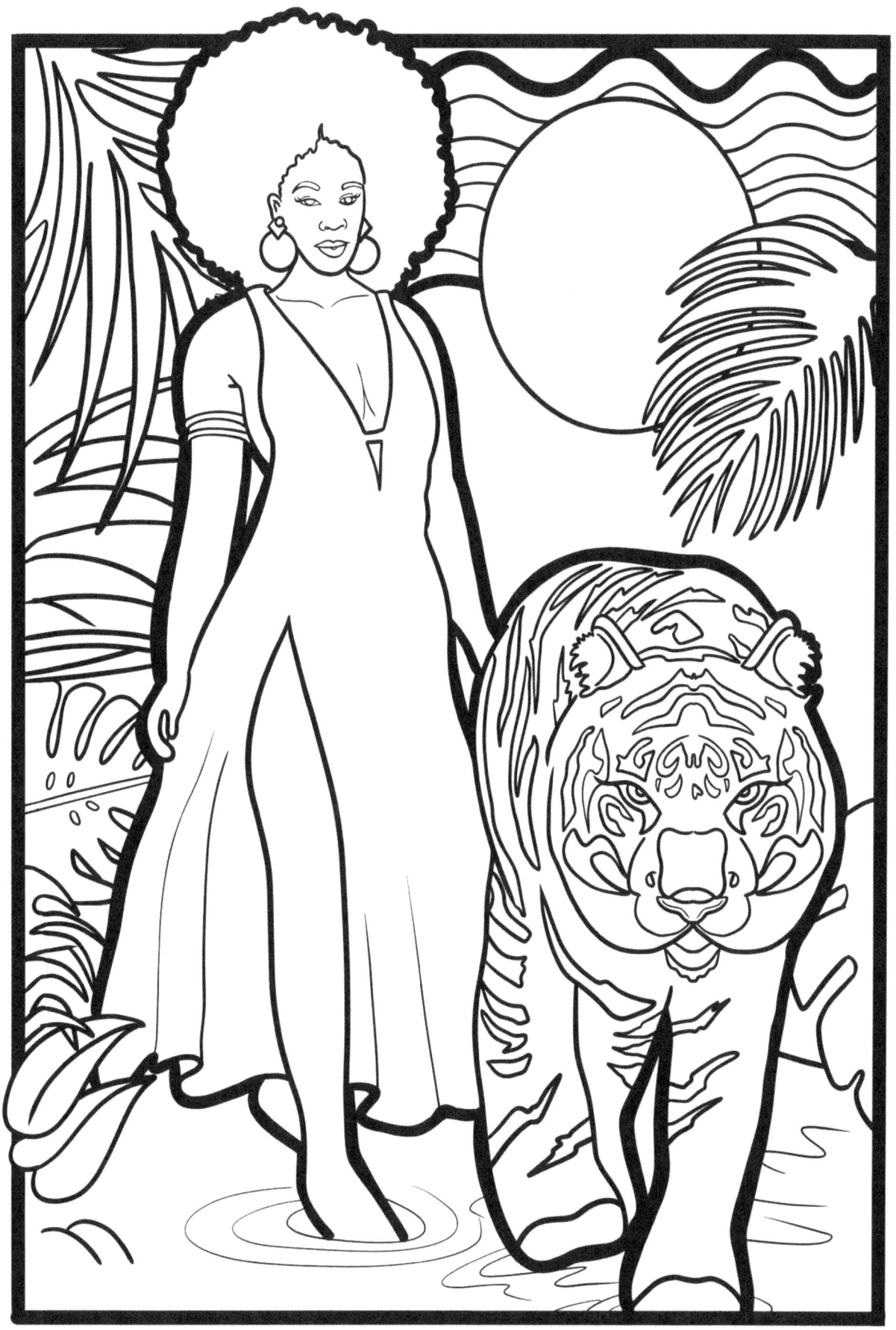

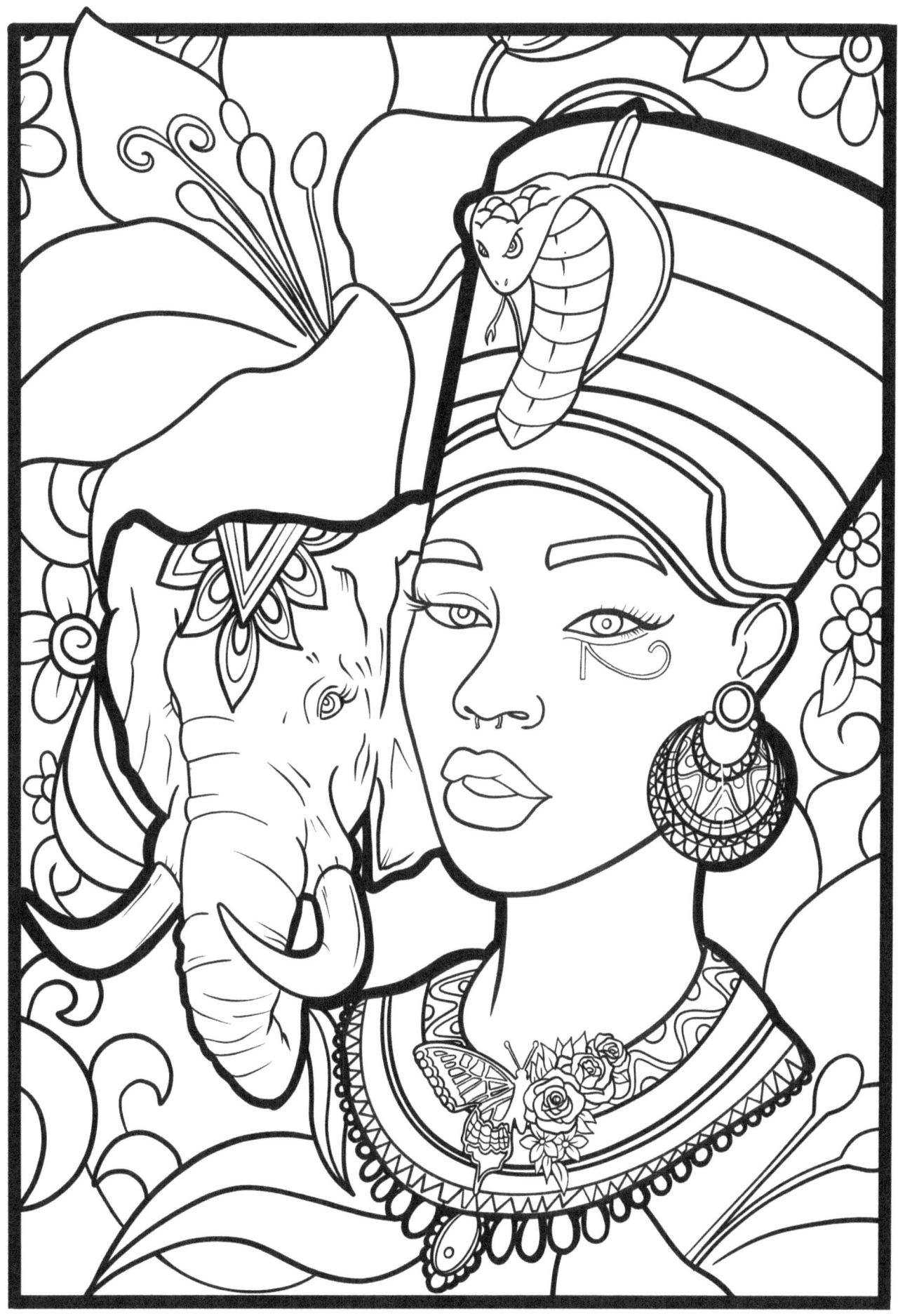

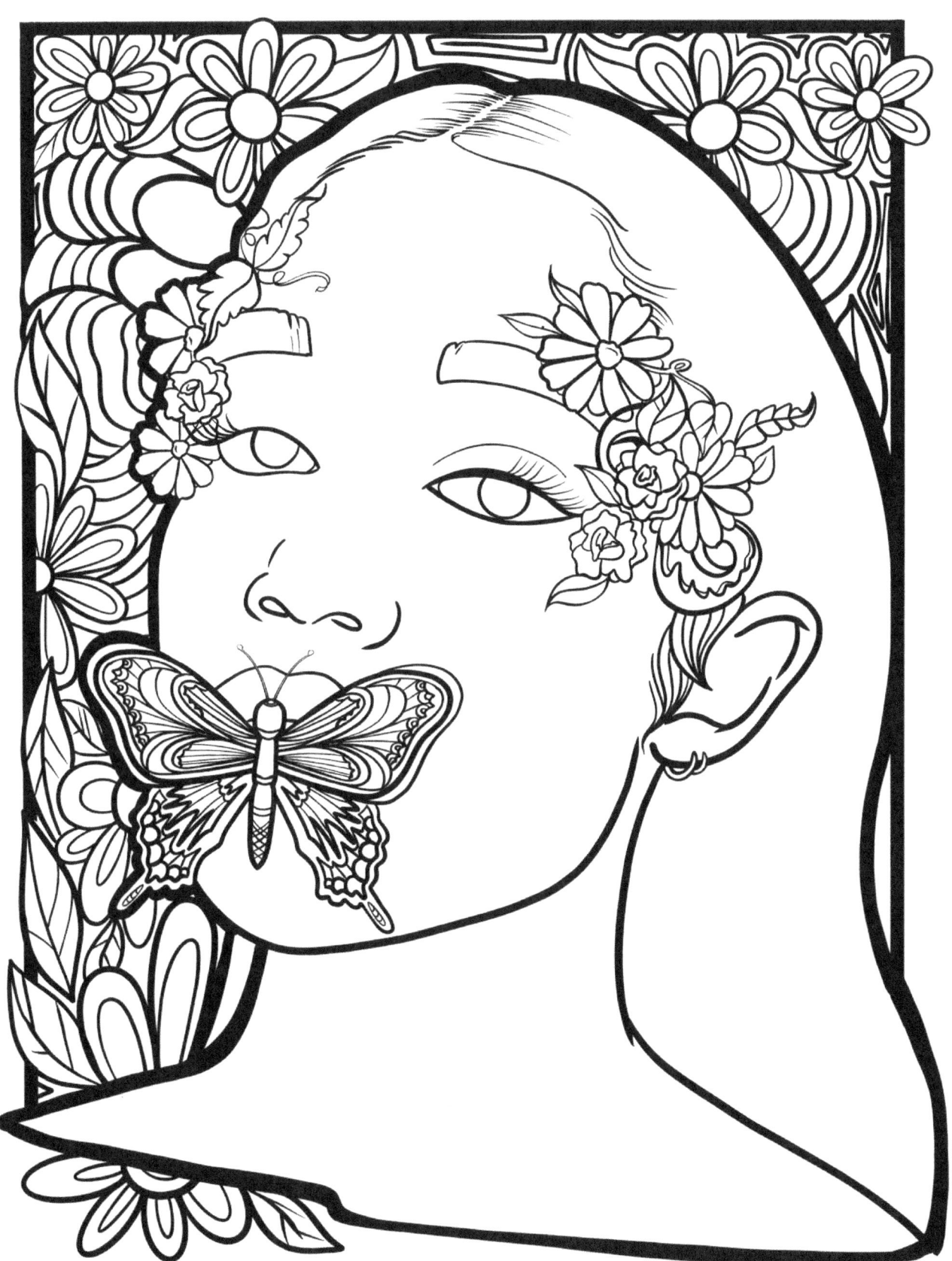

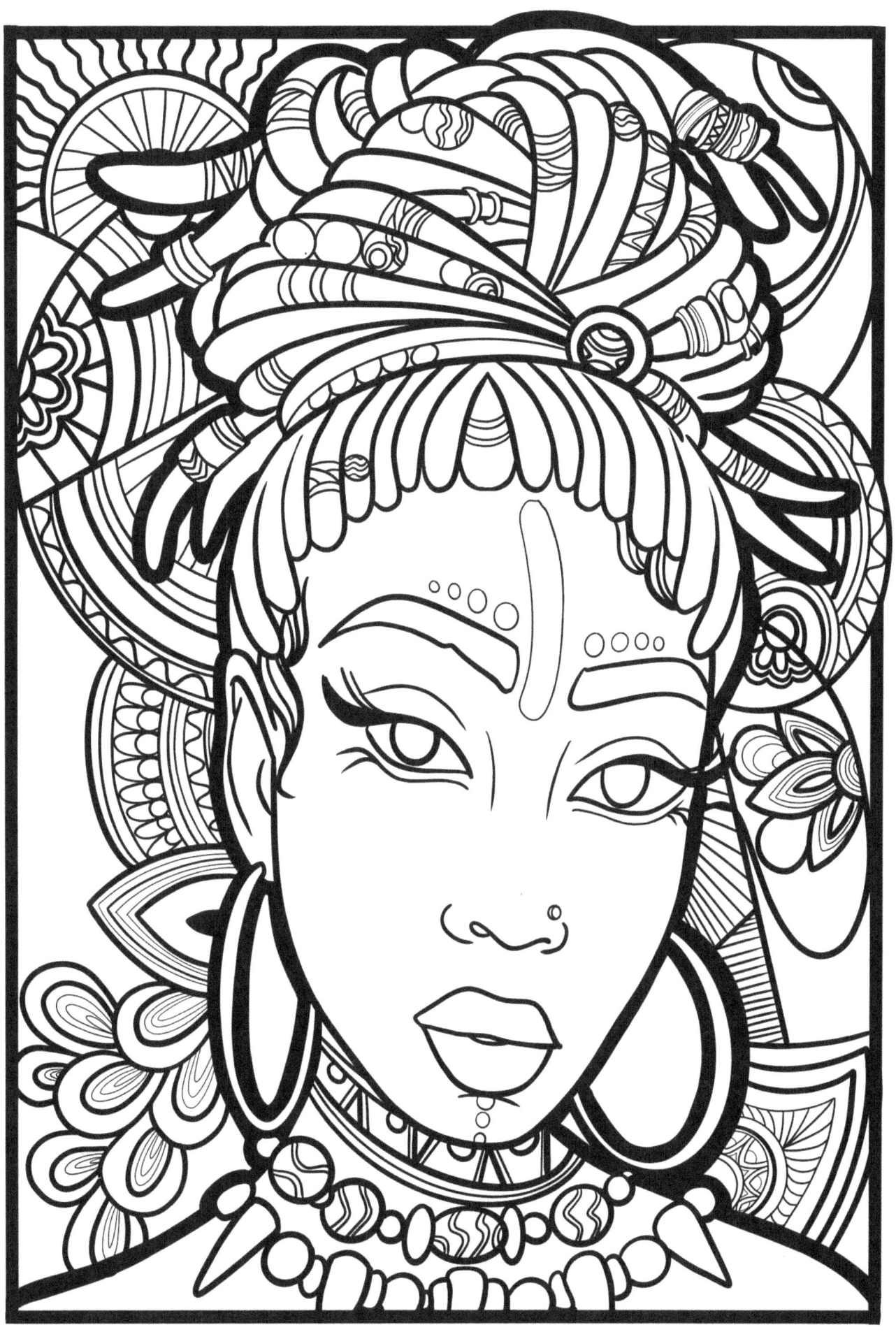

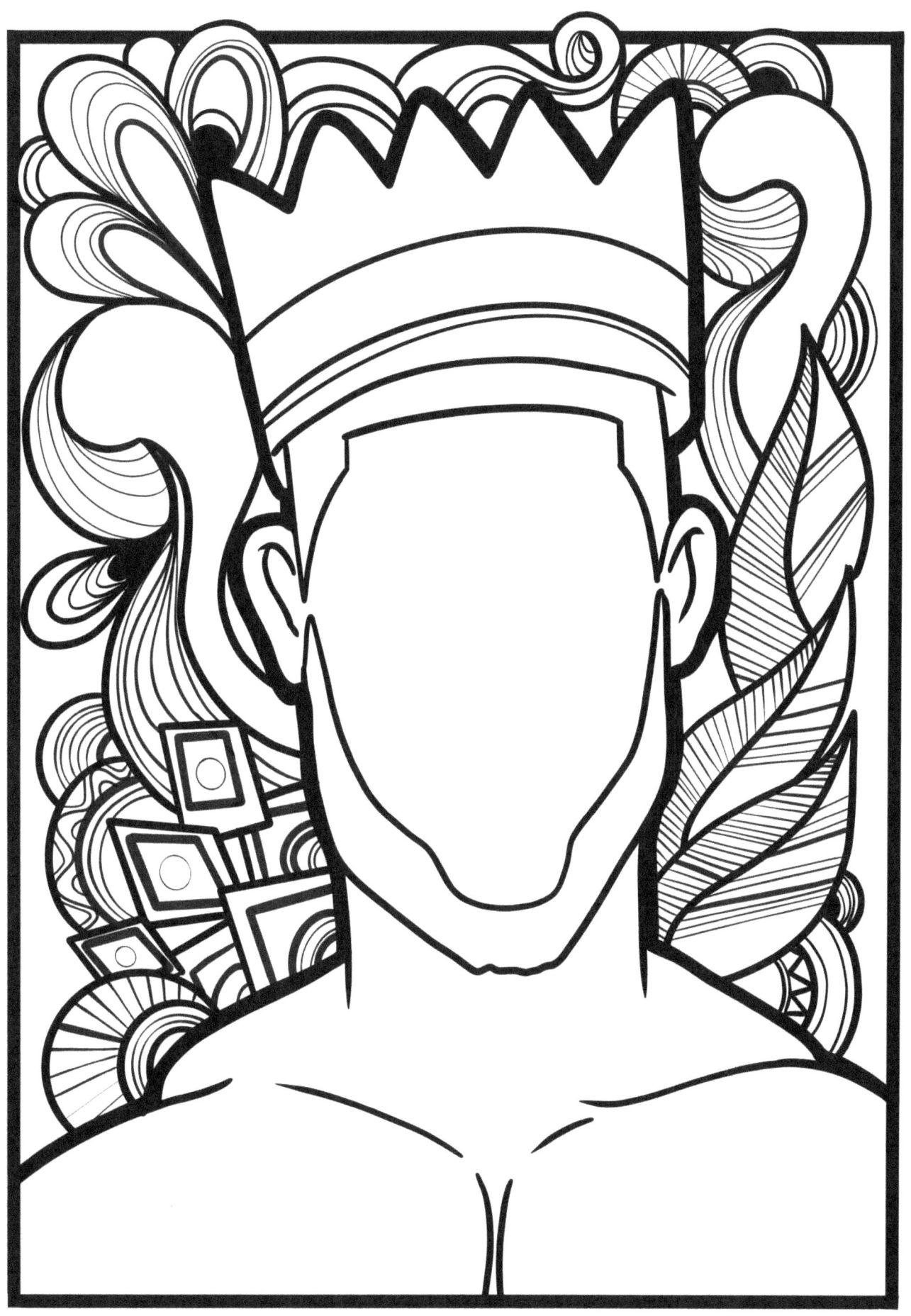

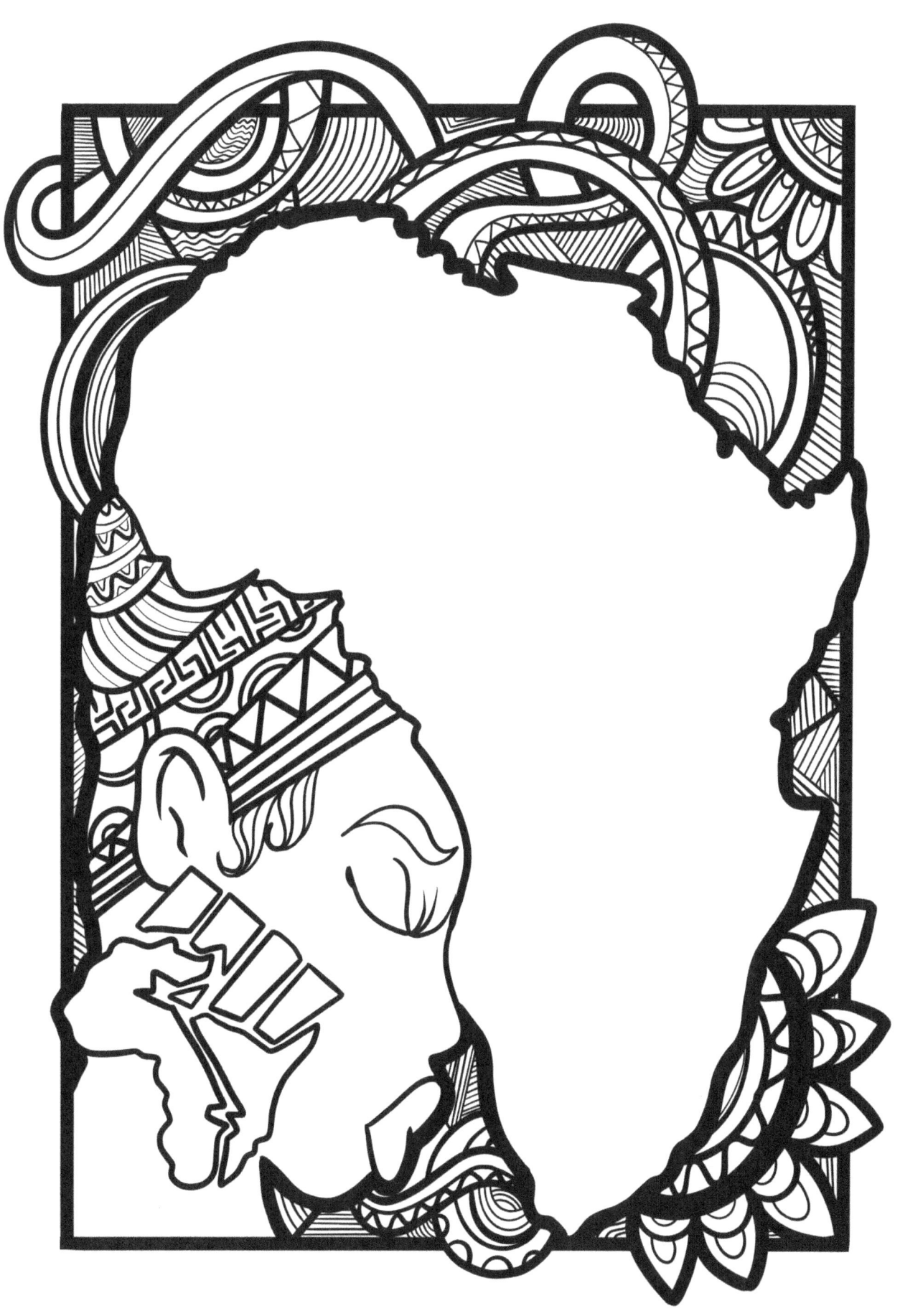

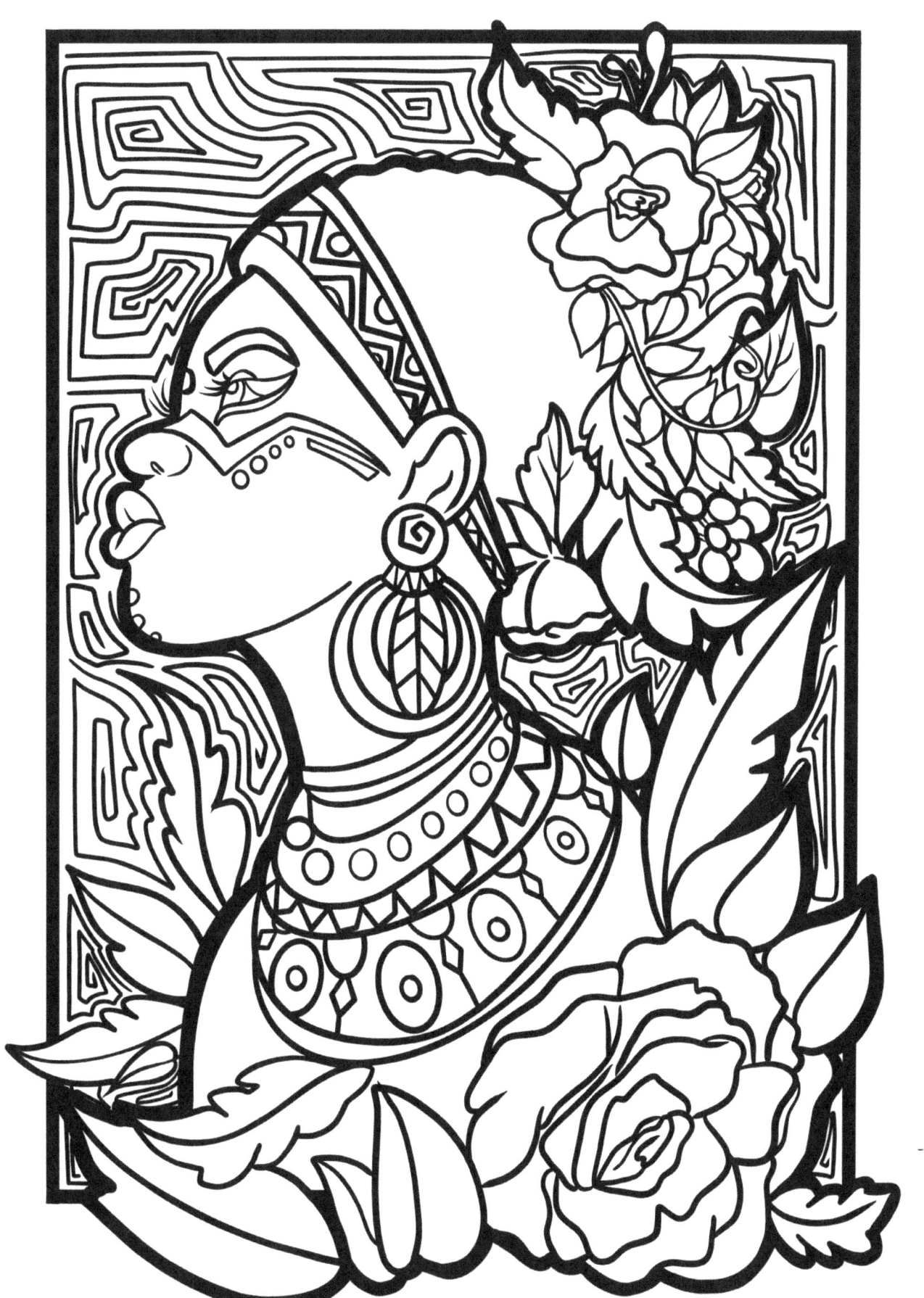

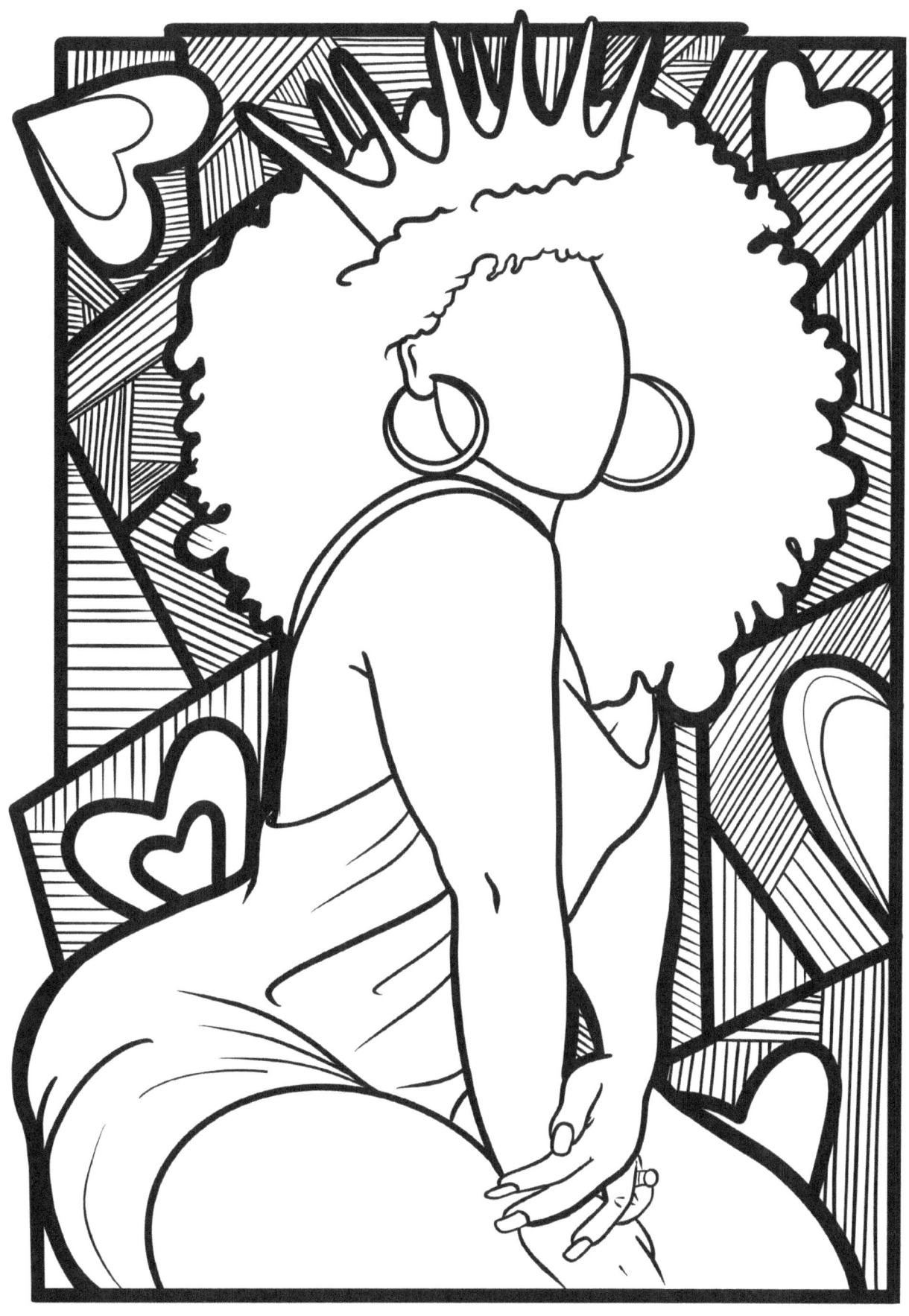

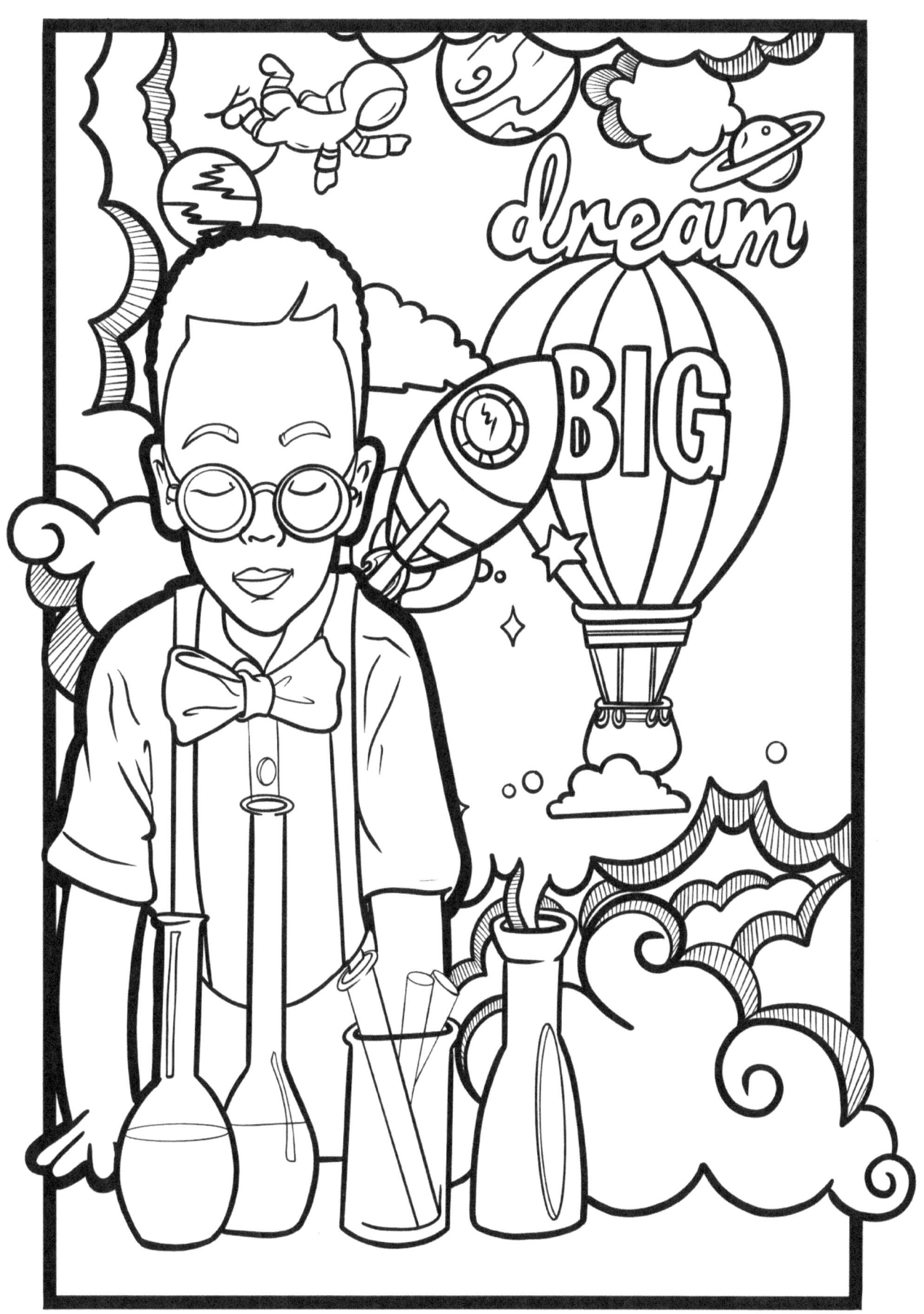

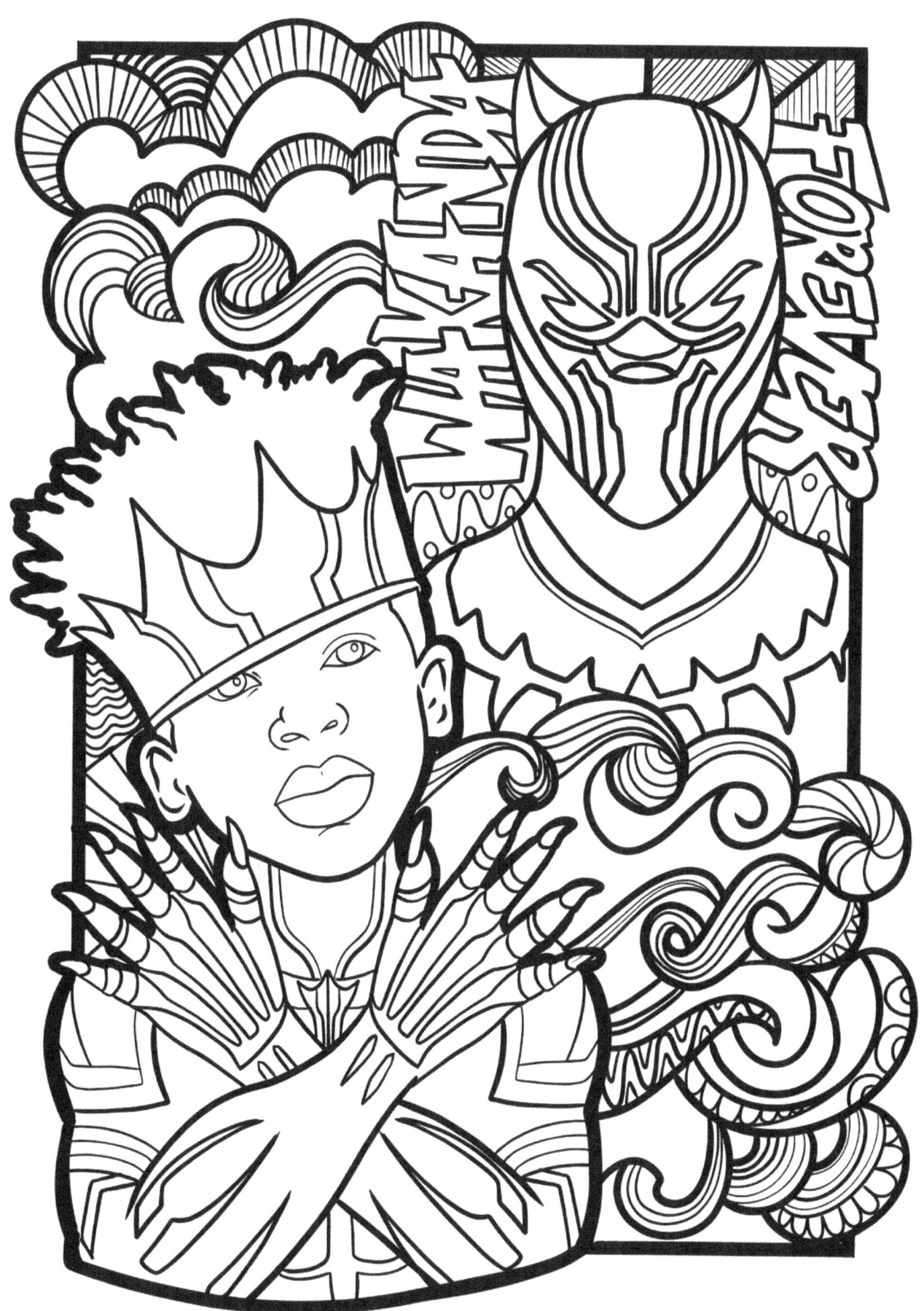

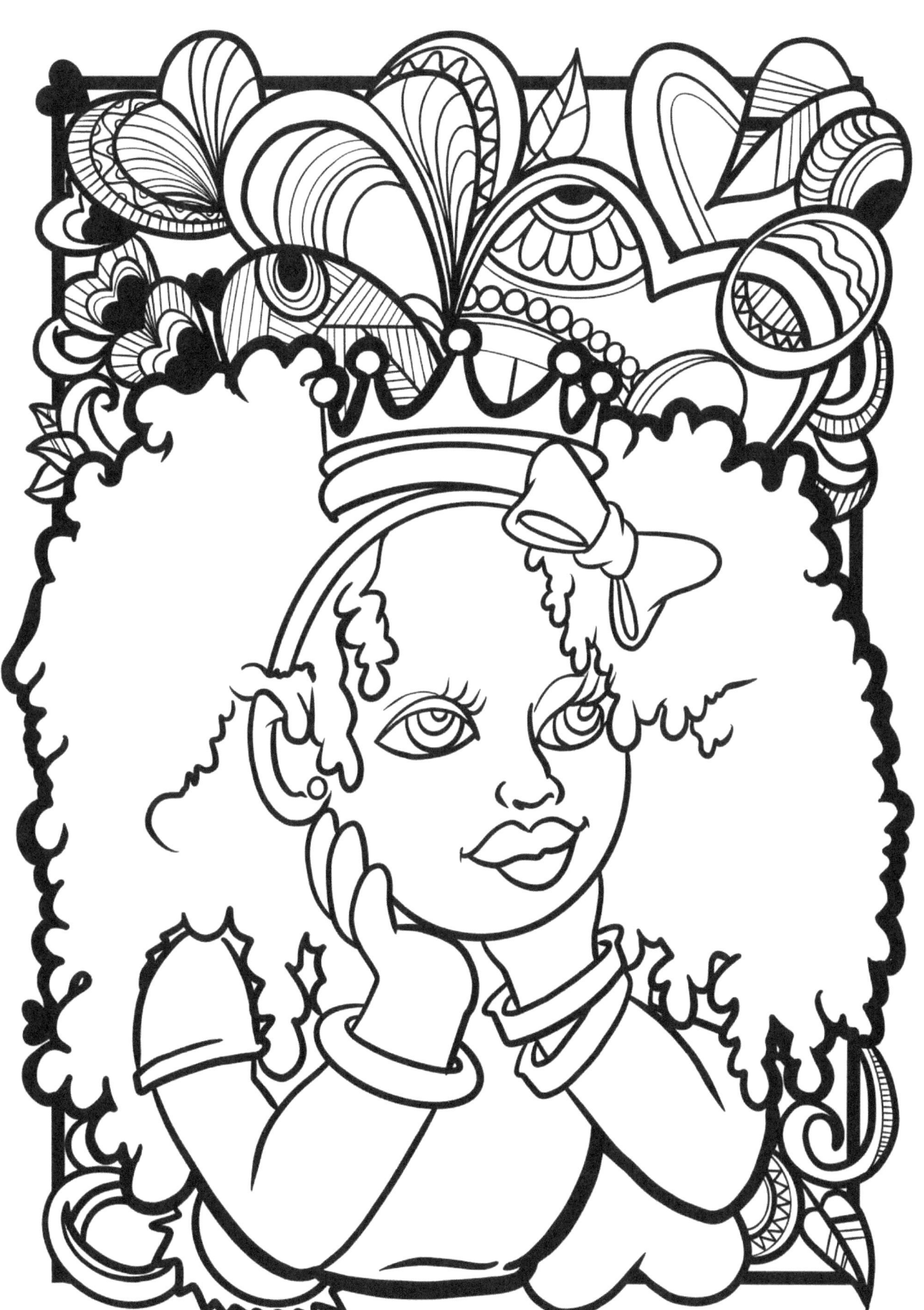

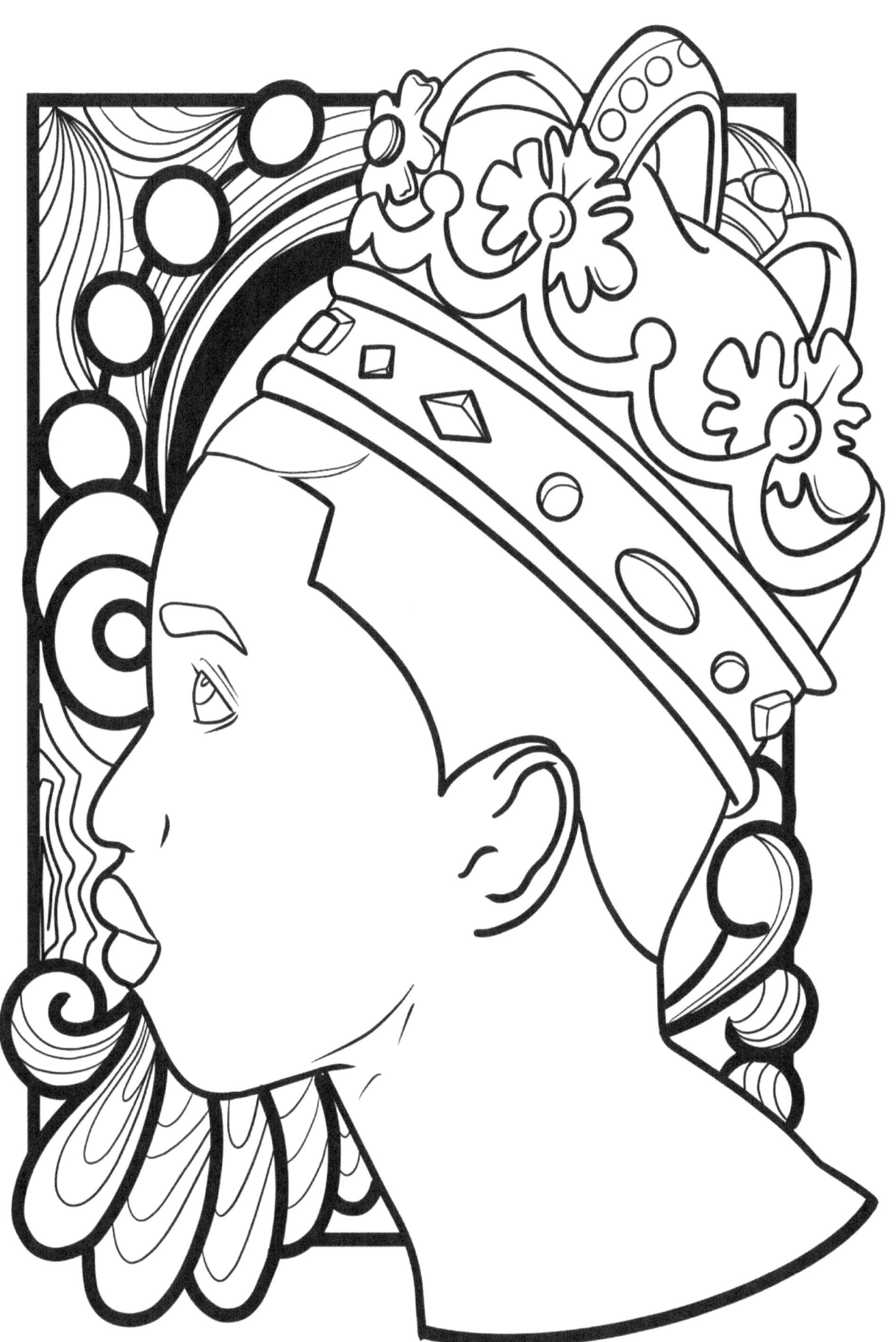

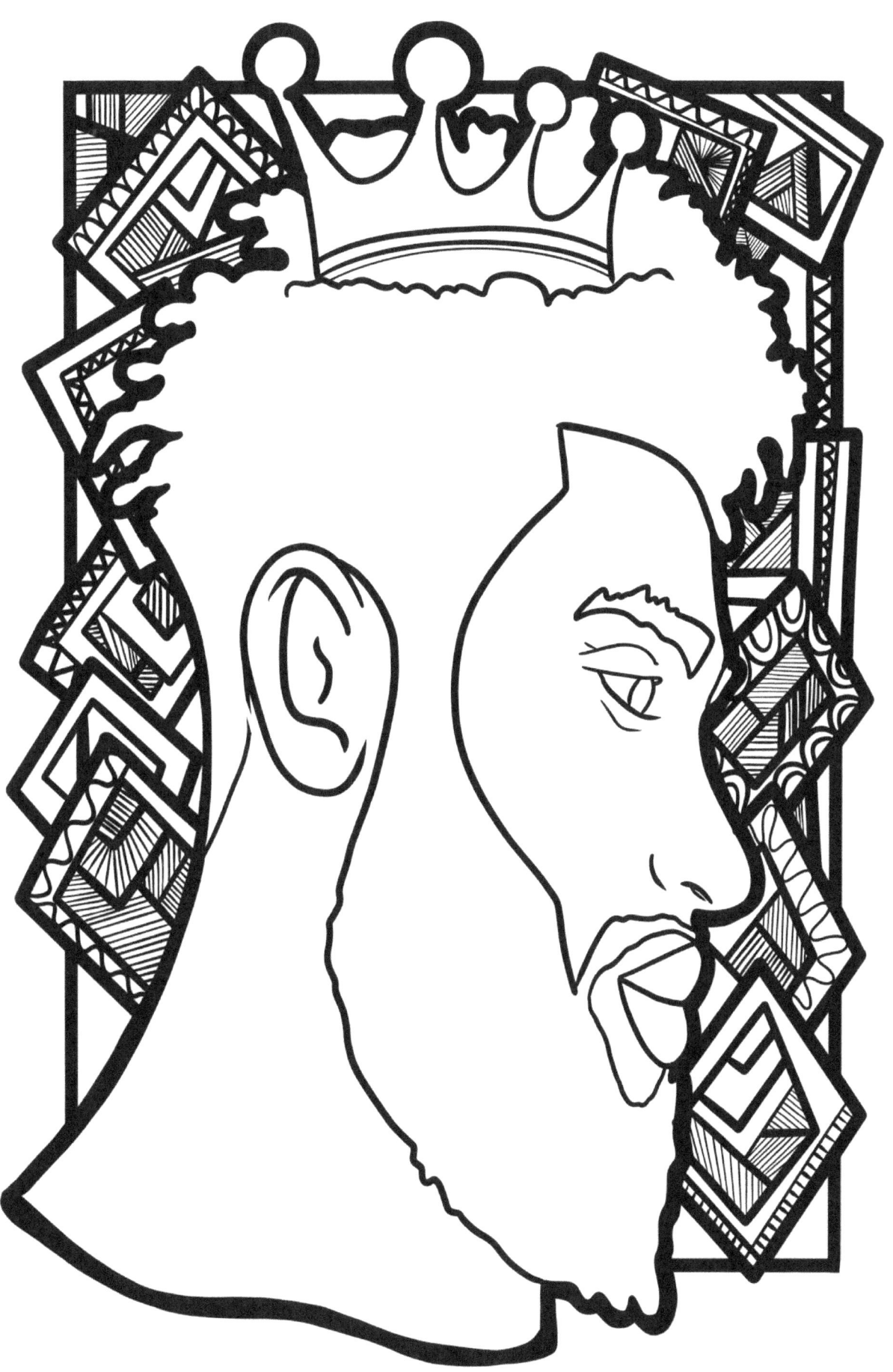

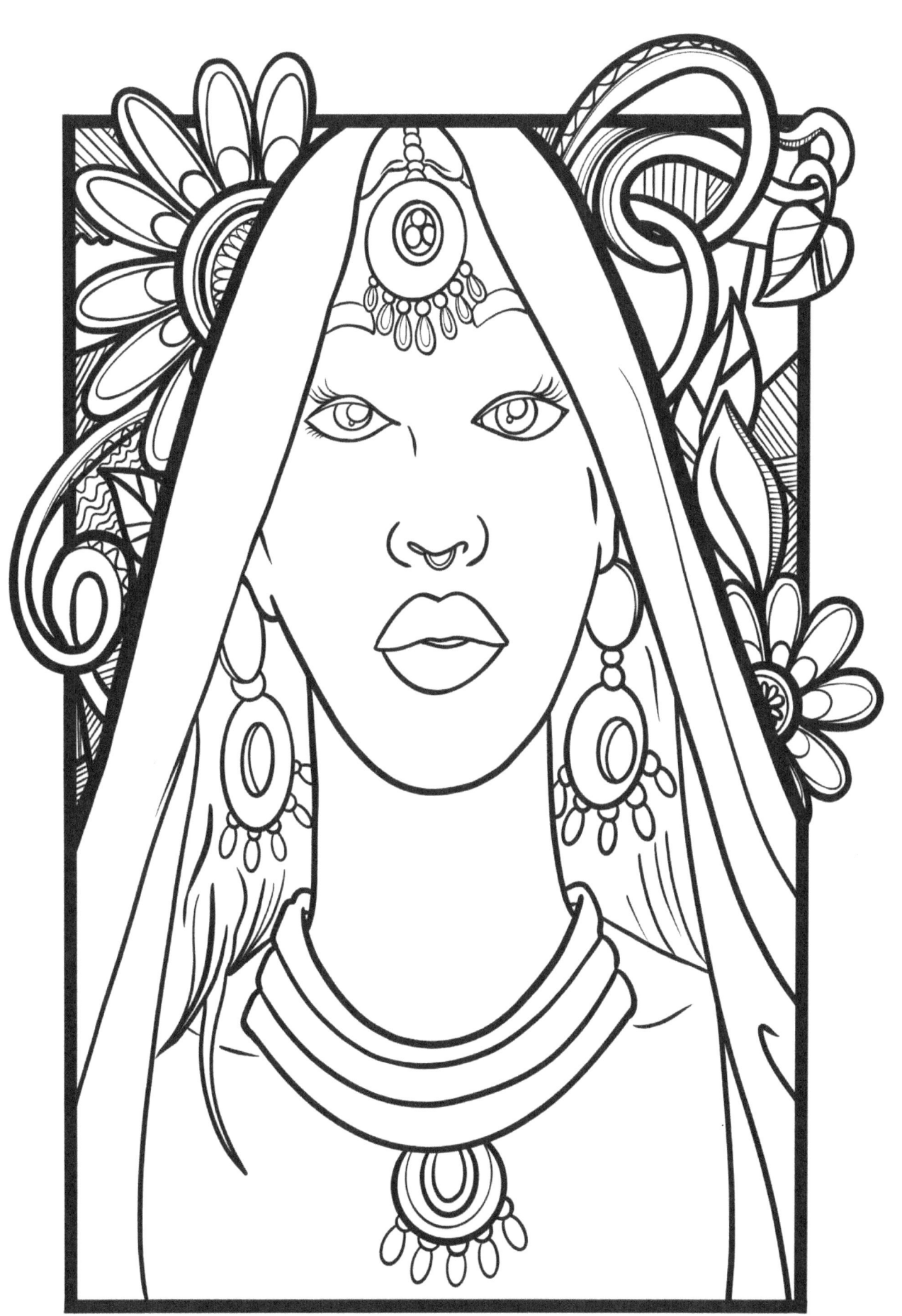

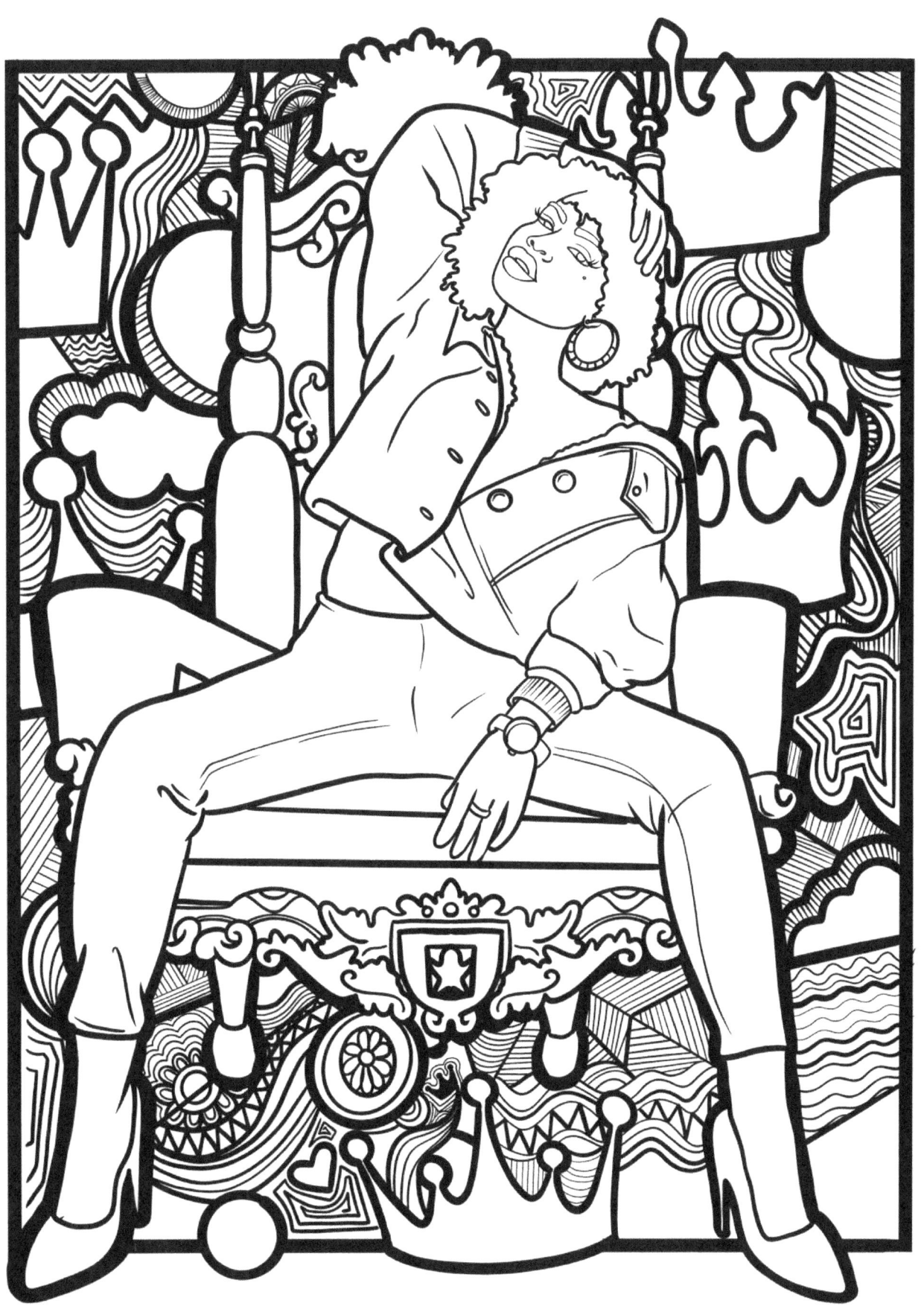

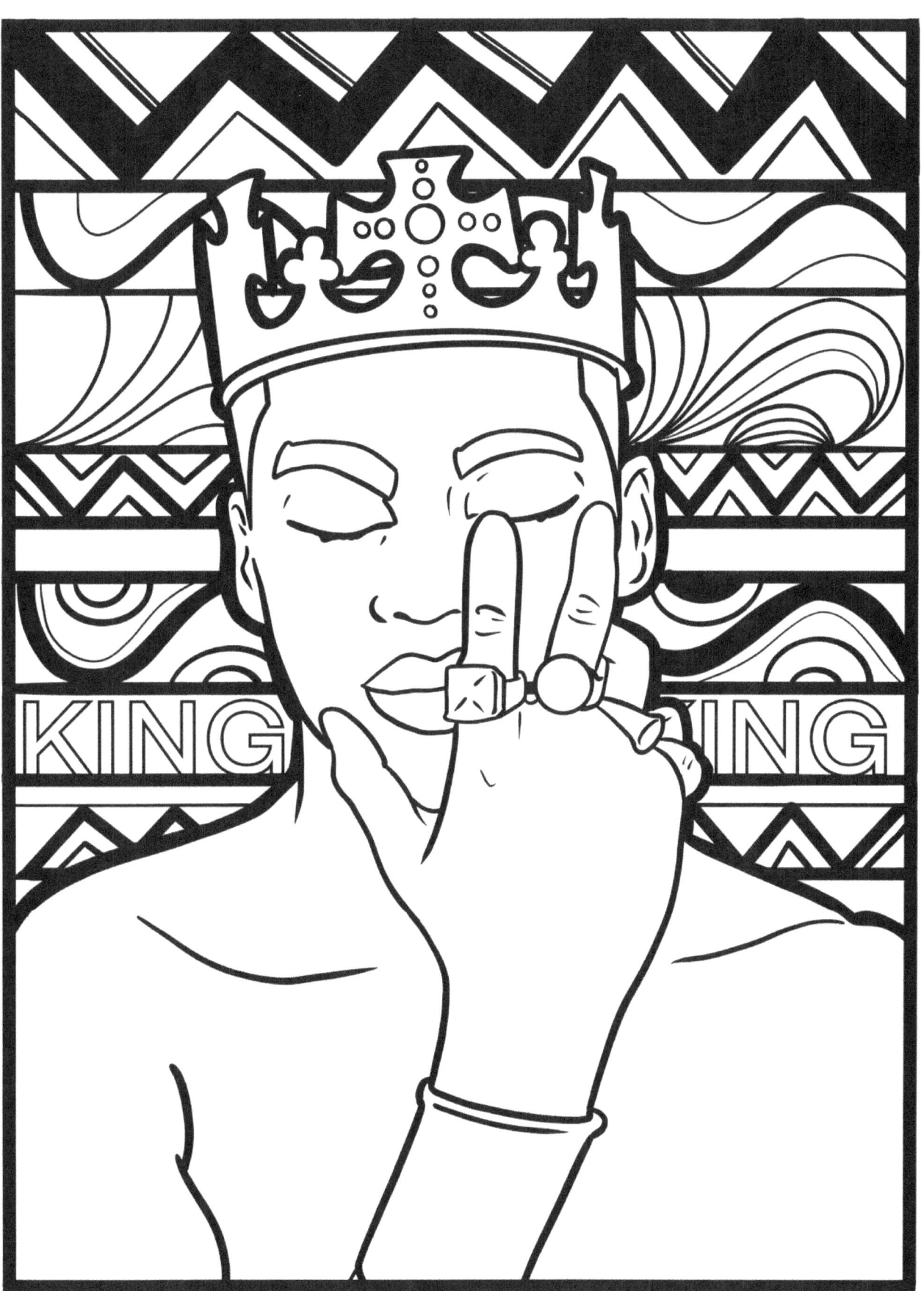

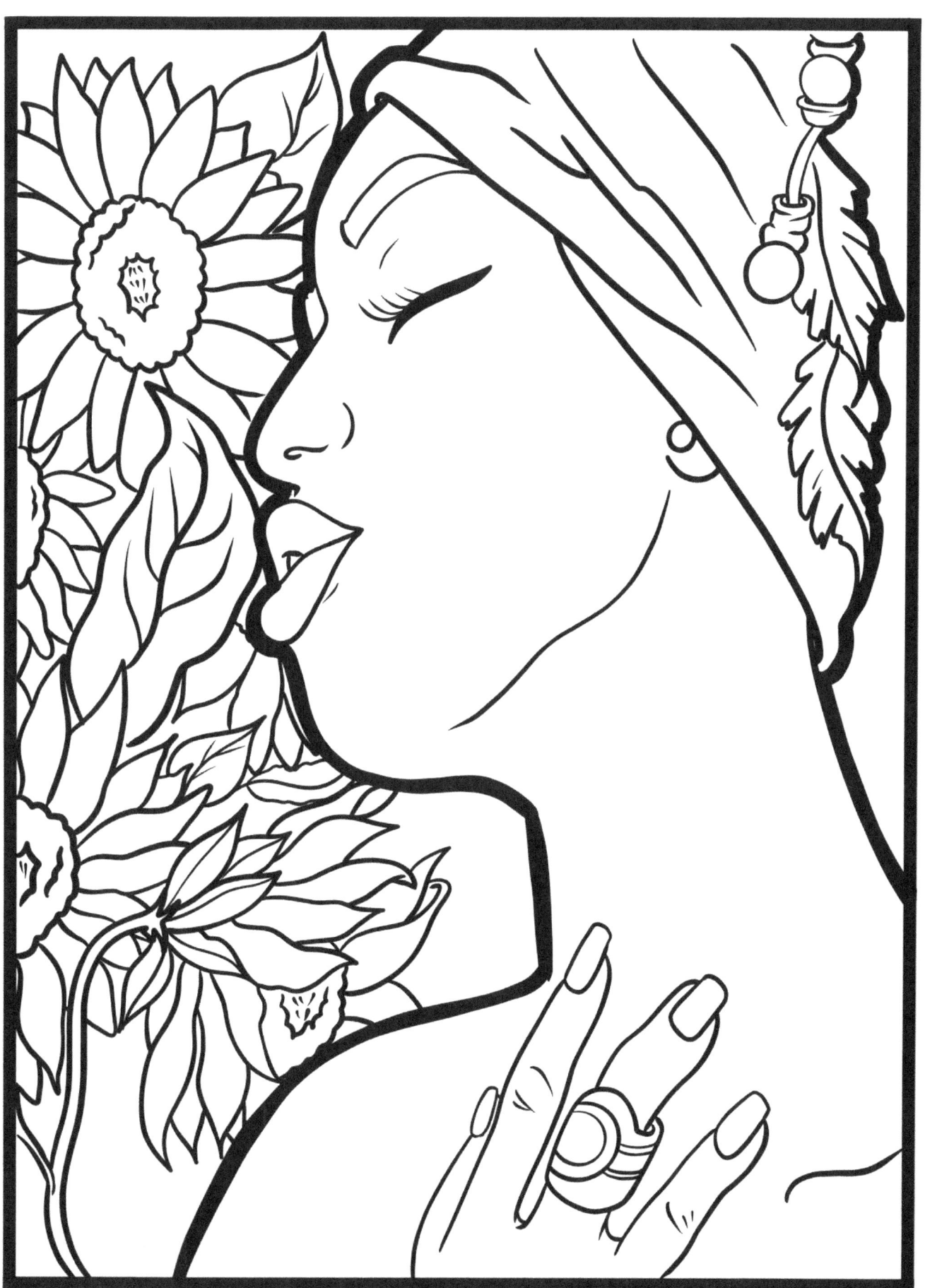

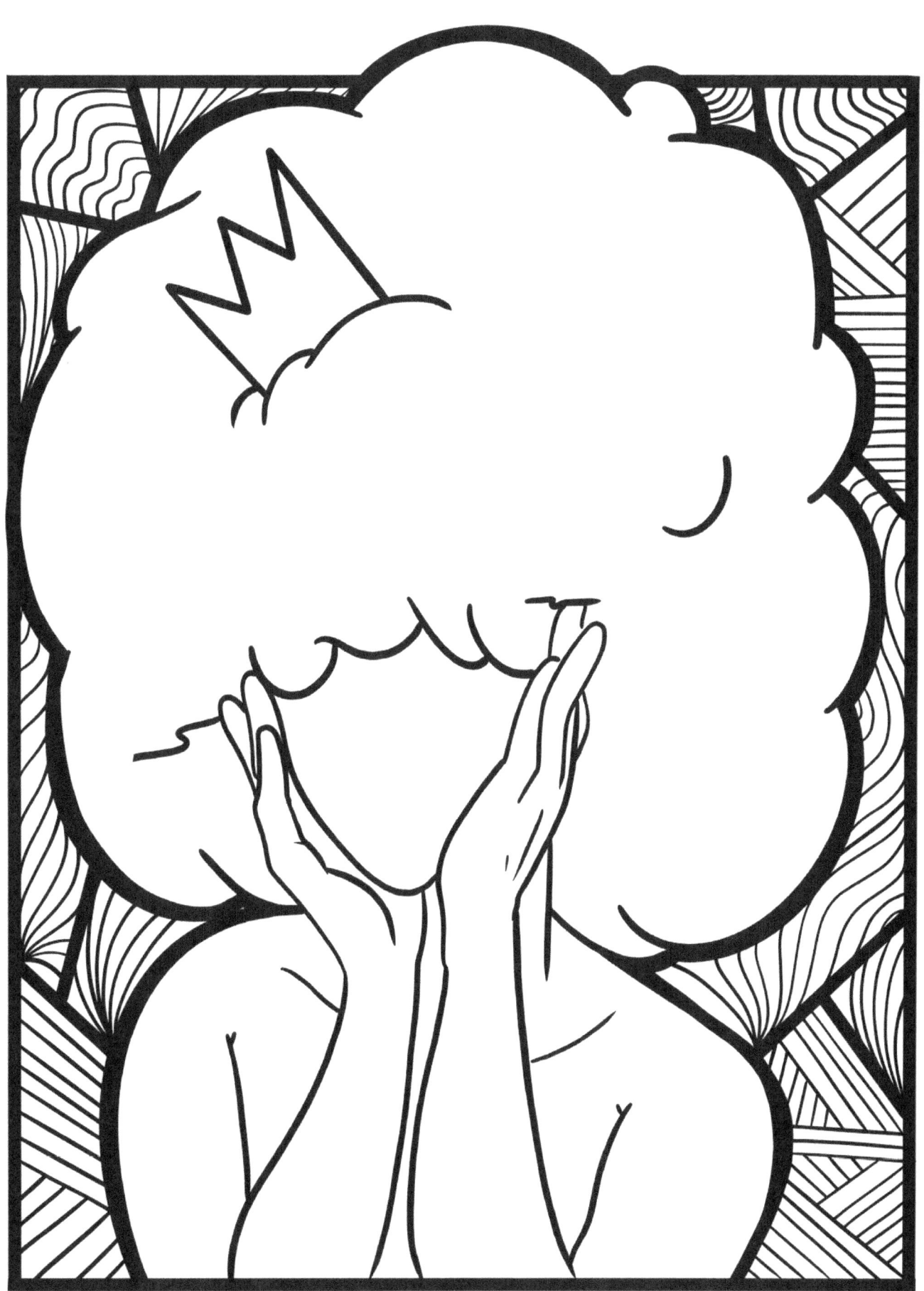

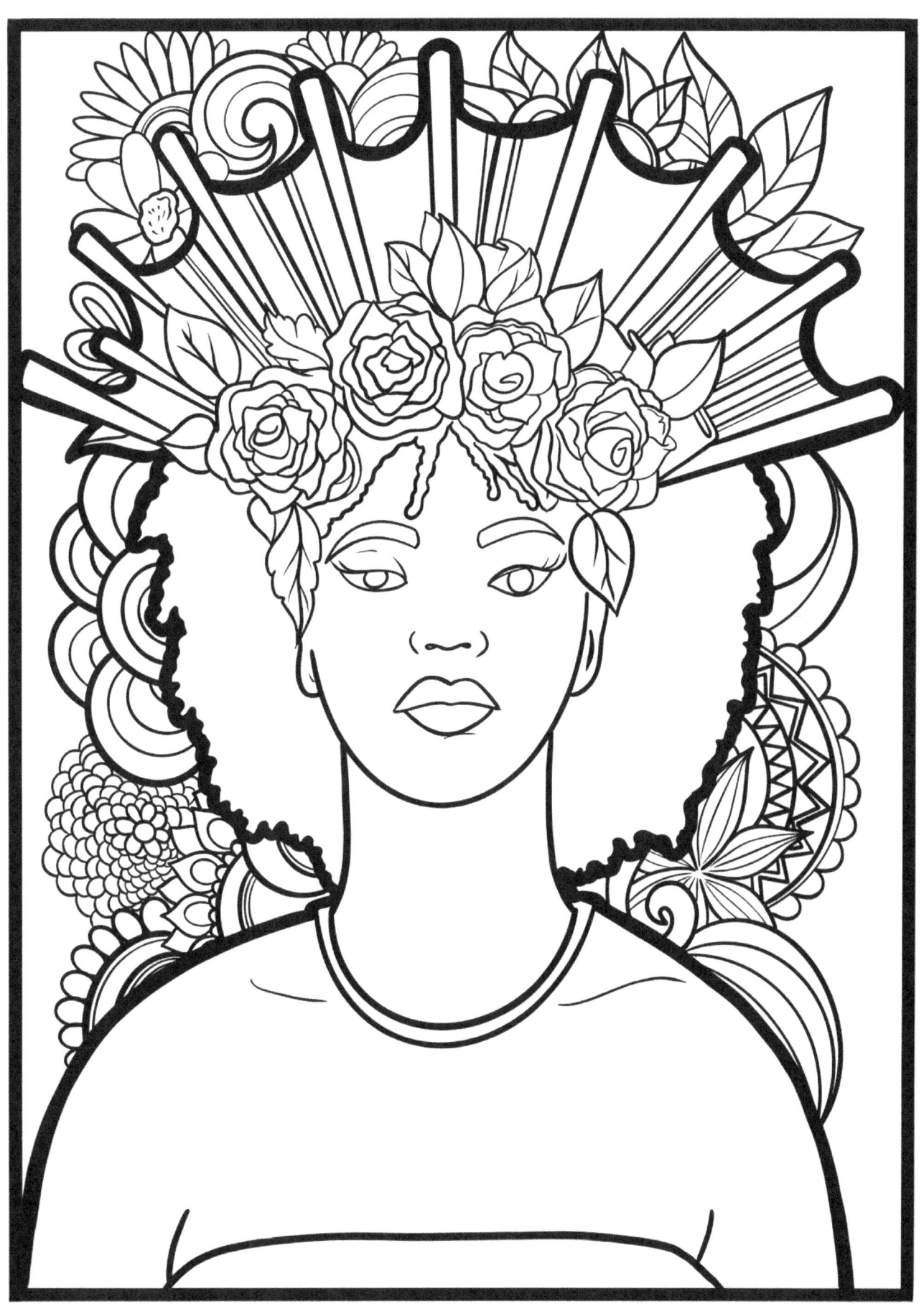

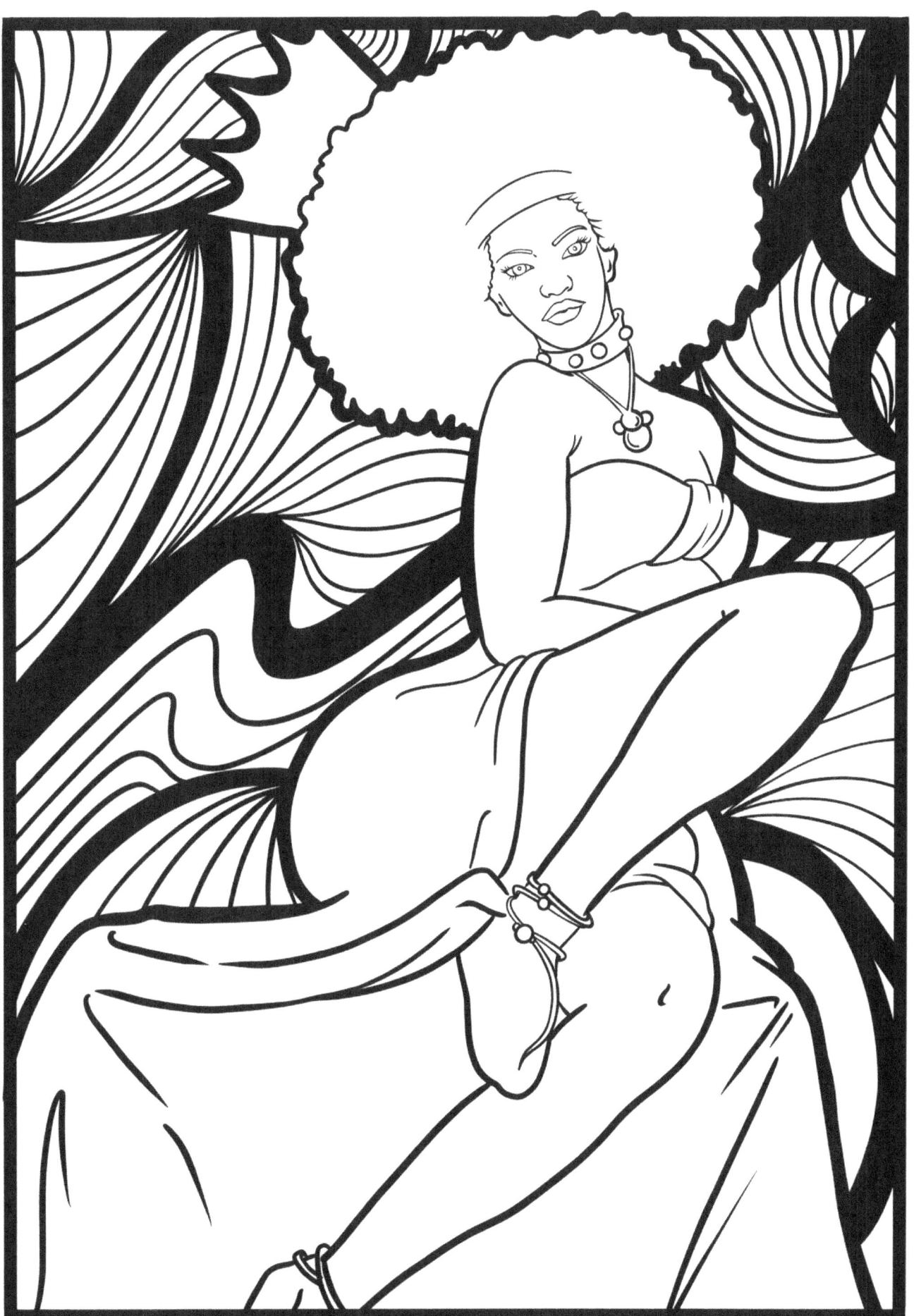

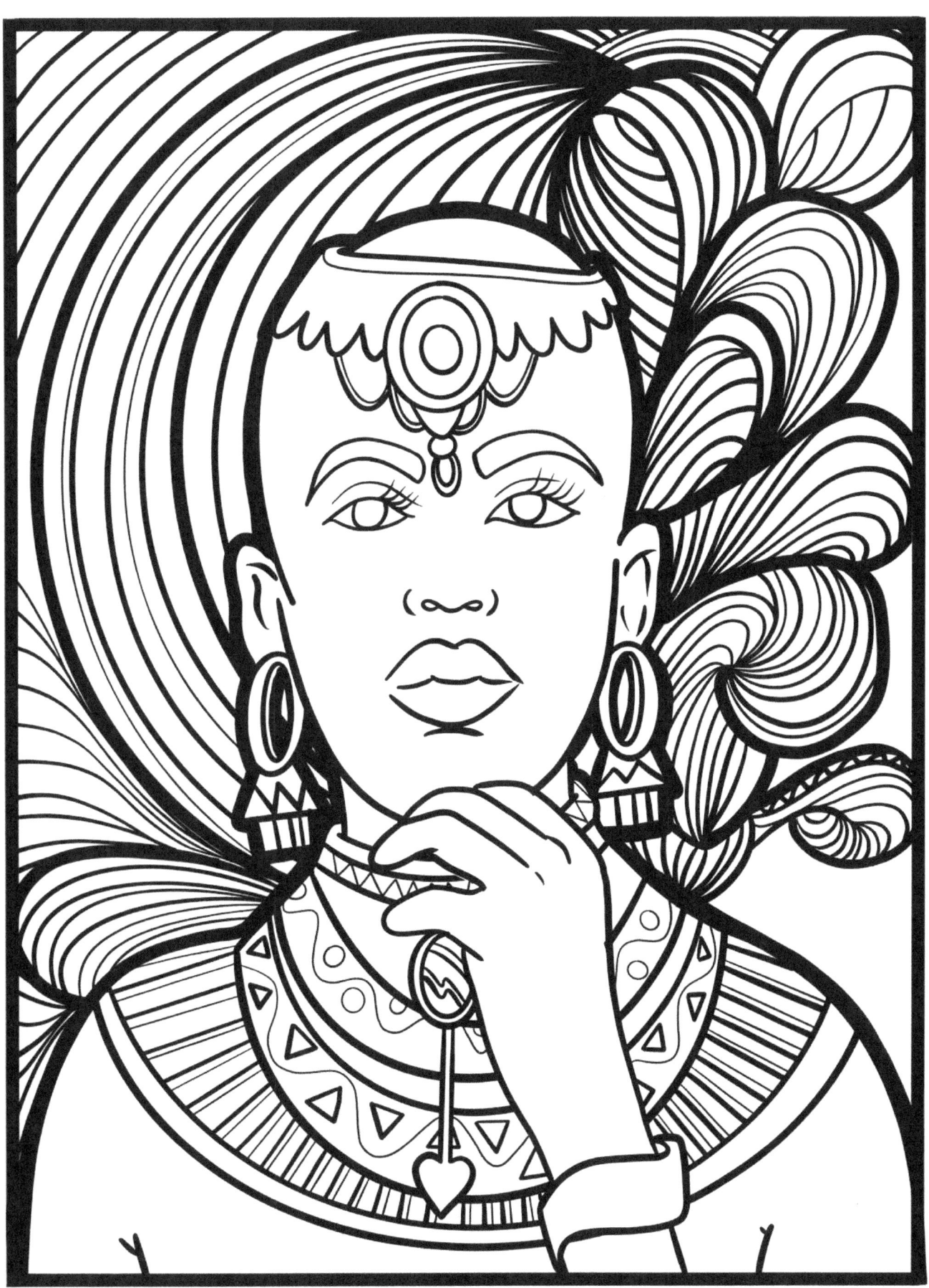

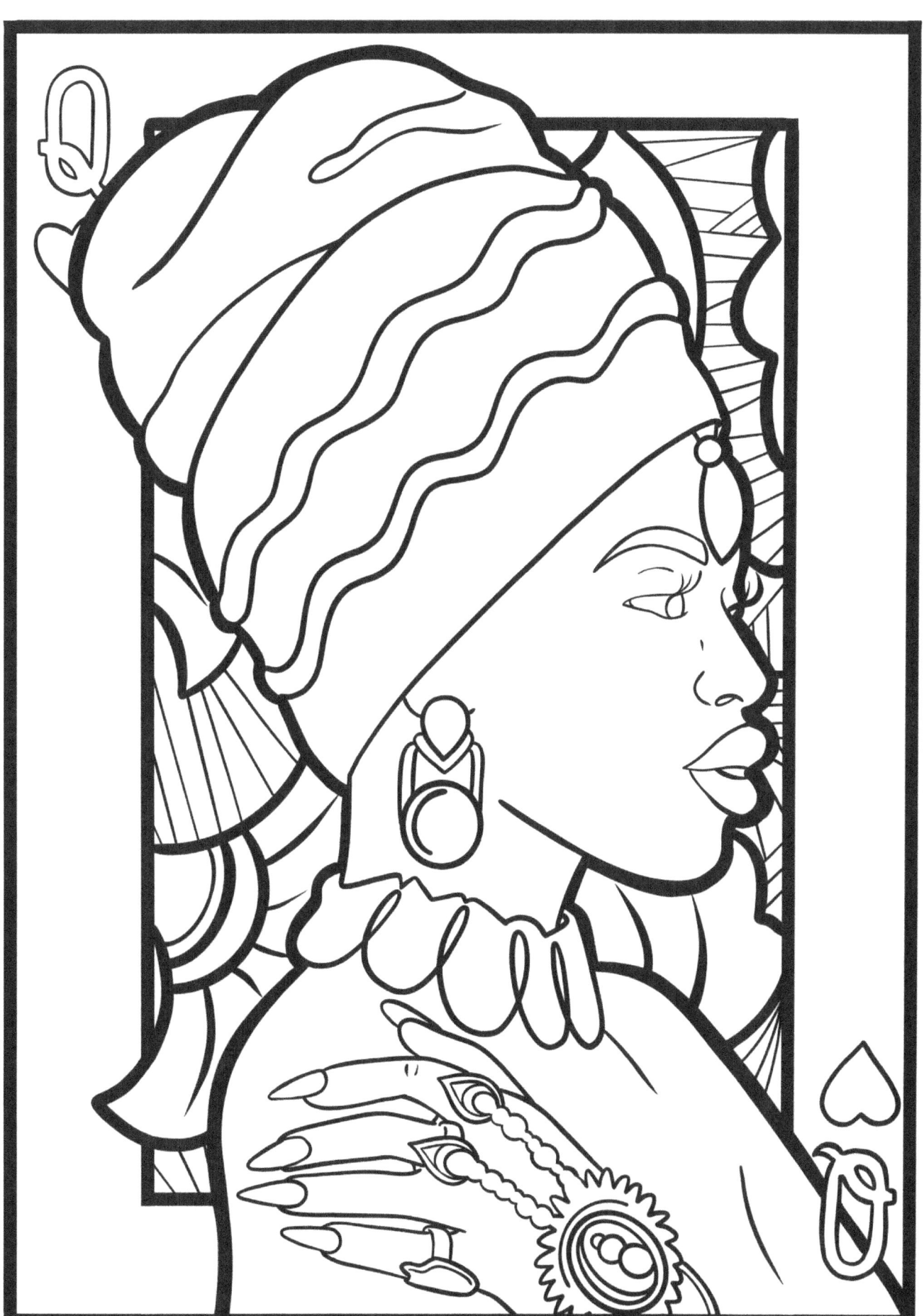

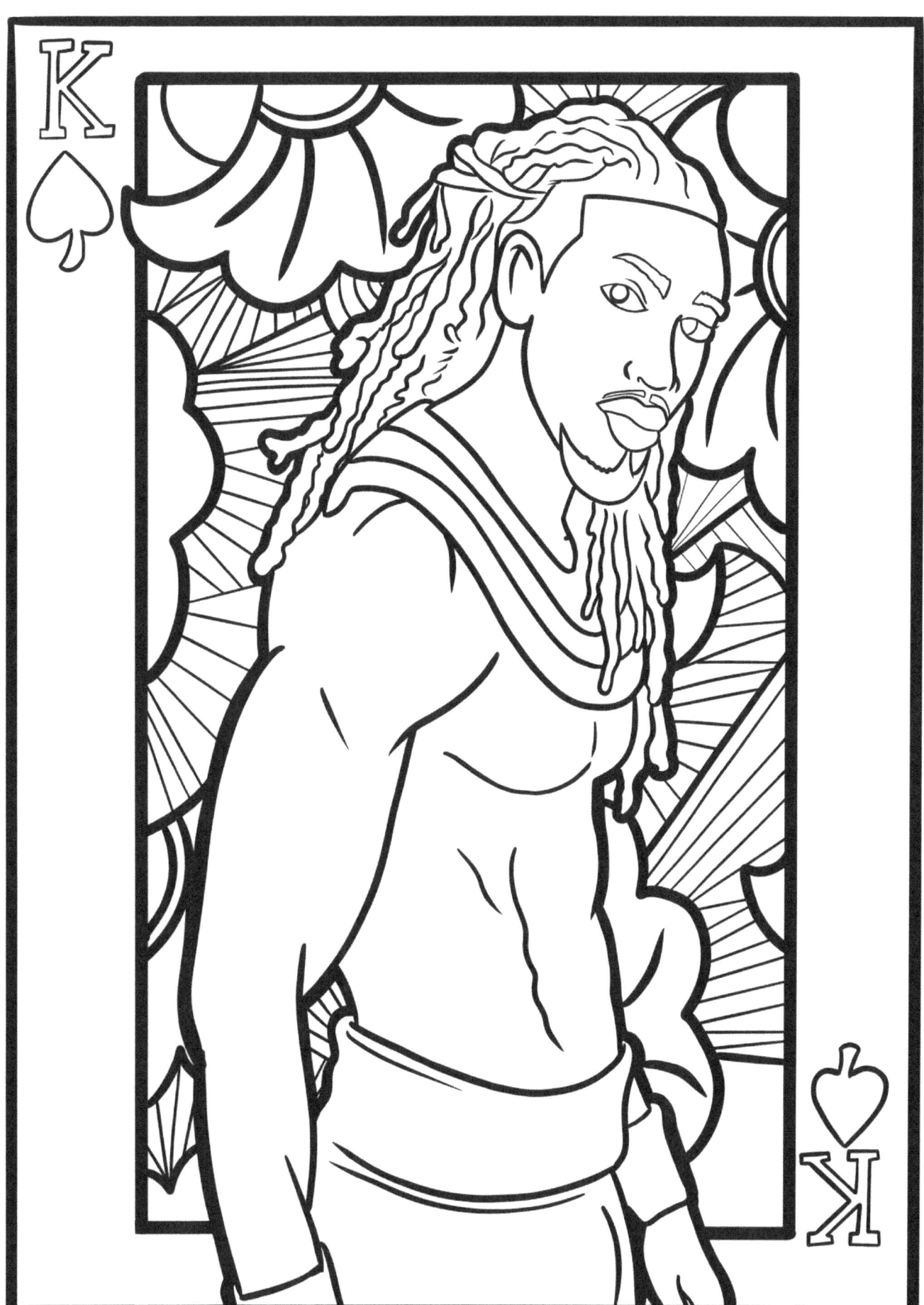